THE HARD WAY:
A DOCTOR'S FIGHT AGAINST ADDICTION, POVERTY, AND DEPRESSION

Jason Ramirez, MD

ISBN: 1548244384
ISBN 13: 9781548244385
Library of Congress Control Number: 2017910132
CreateSpace Independent Publishing Platform
North Charleston, South Carolina

CONTENTS

INTRODUCTION

As the February air ventilated my lungs, with each chilling breath, I pondered how good my life had become. I had a luxury home, the career of my dreams, and a beautiful, loving wife. At the end of a busy workday at a family-medicine office in Carlisle, Pennsylvania, I reflected on the patients I had seen throughout the day. As a family doctor, you never know what to expect from the day, but this had been a typical day with the pace hastened by a steady flow of sore throats, high blood pressure, diabetic-care appointments, well-child visits, and routine physical exams.

The commute on Interstate 81 found traffic lighter than usual, allowing me to arrive home several minutes earlier than I typically would. As I pulled into the driveway, I was excited to share my good day with my wife. I entered the powder room to find the house unusually clean and quiet.

"How was your day, love?" The look of trepidation on my wife's face told me there was much more to this question than the simple inquiry would suggest.

"Sit over here." Her voice quavered as she gestured to our love seat warmed by a stone fireplace five feet away. Without saying a word, I obeyed her request, expecting the worst. Seconds seemed to draw out into minutes until the silence was broken by my wife's cracking voice. "I'm pregnant."

I could not acknowledge anything after that, as my brain failed to register any further words Melissa had spoken. For my poor wife, the second period of complete silence must have seemed like an eternity. I don't know if I visualized the wall I stared at for a reported five minutes or how I maneuvered my body upstairs to our master bedroom, but I went into hibernation for the next fourteen hours. When I arose, I went downstairs to find Melissa sitting on the living room couch. She appeared scared to hear me speak, yet her eyes pleaded for the silence to break.

"Did we have a conversation when I got home from work yesterday? Something about having a baby?" I asked. Indeed, we had. I had not had a dream. I was going to be a father.

I was content living a life without children—not because of a dislike for them but rather due to a fear of not being a good father. Though we never discussed starting a family, Melissa was aware of my concerns. She knew I'd had a challenging childhood, unlike hers, which had been based on strong family ties and values. I knew my childhood experience was the source of my fear. Now I had to face that fear head on, and I had no idea how I was going to do it.

Seven years and two children later, my life could not be better, nor would I change it for anything; I love being a parent. My family consists of my beautiful wife, Melissa Anne; our son, Alexander Louis; and daughter, Olivia Violet Ramirez. Alex is my absolute mini-me. A friend once commented that it looked like I was thrown into a dryer and out popped Alex. Olivia looks just as adorable as her mother, and the joy she has brought to our lives is indescribable. My wife, Melissa, is my soul mate, my foundation for happiness, and, as I will detail, my savior.

Marrying Melissa and having a family provided me with a solid foundation for the first time in my life, a foundation that has allowed me to reach professional goals I never thought possible. I now flourish in academic family medicine as an assistant professor at the University of Maryland School of Medicine, where I function as the residency-program director for the Department of Family and Community Medicine.

My road to personal and professional success has been anything but easy or traditional. On a road paved by parental heroin addiction, homelessness, and major depressive disorder, many obstacles have threatened my success and my life. Fortunately, I have transformed from an angry and bitter young man who prided himself on beating the odds on his own to a mature husband and father who acknowledges the influence of the many caring people who contributed to my success. My intent is that souls will be touched by the pages that follow. May they give hope to all those who feel they cannot achieve their dreams because life is too hard. I believe all of us can achieve our goals and aspirations through a relentless work ethic, a little help, and faith that no matter how hopeless things may appear, persistence and dedication will pay off.

ACKNOWLEDGEMENTS

To my parents-through all their struggles they did not give up on their children. The lessons learned from them may not have been intentional but I learned to work hard for everything I wanted and to never give up.

To the many supporters who took a chance on a teenager they barely knew. I thank you for seeing in me the potential to succeed. I hope I have made you proud.

Most importantly, thank you to my beautiful wife, Melissa Ramirez. Without her unconditional and unwavering love I would not have had the strength to go on in life. She has blessed me with two incredible children- Alexander Louis and Olivia Violet Ramirez. Both keep me young and full of life. Because of Melissa, Alexander and Olivia, I now enjoy a happy life. No longer living it *The Hard Way*!

THE ORIGINS OF THE RAMIREZ FAMILY

I have always envisioned my mother as a beautiful young woman on the day she met my father. Robin Elizabeth Tuller was fourteen years of age when she was approached by a handsome young man one summer day. Daniel Louis Ramirez was a twenty-four-year-old Puerto Rican man with no fear. As the story goes, Danny approached the young woman and asked for a dime to make a phone call. The rest is history, as the bad-boy persona of my father was enough to win my mother's heart from that day forth.

My mother was one of seven children, all raised by her mother without much support. I never learned much about my mother's childhood. I know she did well in school and was frequently an A student, a fact that never surprised me, as I always thought of my mother as a very intelligent person. I believe she could have been anything she wanted in life if she had pursued an education. Instead, she dropped out of high school in the tenth grade. To her credit, she did earn her GED and completed two years at a community college, earning an associate's degree in accounting.

My father, an only child raised by his mother, grew up on the streets of New York City. My father and his mother never got along, and without the guidance of a male figure in his life, my dad took to the streets to find acceptance and a sense of belonging. He was educated by the Catholic school system until he dropped out of high school in the tenth grade. Not appreciating the value of education, he took to the streets, using his fast fists and sharp tongue to survive. Unfortunately, he fell victim to the disorder of addiction, a condition that would ultimately lead to his premature death.

I have been told I was blessed with the spiritual gift of service to others, a gift I was using prior to my entry into this world. At the young and impressionable age of fifteen, my mother was head over heels in love with my twenty-five-year-old father. The ten-year gap meant nothing to them, and for better or worse, they were determined to be together. The barrier was the fact that my mother was a minor, and in 1972, the state of Connecticut did not allow the marriage of an adult to a minor unless the couple had an off-spring together. My parents obliged the courts, and on September 26, 1973, I, Jason Alexander Ramirez, was born. Conceived by intention, I assisted my parents in getting married. My service to humanity had begun.

By the age of six, I started to recognize that my family was different. I observed that my father had a bad temper. He was quick to get mad, and his anger was taken out on my mother. I witnessed regular episodes of physical abuse. I recall hearing my father screaming at the top of his lungs one evening. My father was not happy that my mother had arrived home late.

Startled, I climbed out of my bed and slowly cracked open my bedroom door. My innocent hazel eyes glazed with fear at the rage that was my father. With intense fury, my father began violently thrusting body shots to my mother's midsection. My defenseless mother, crying in pain, collapsed to the floor. I closed my door and ran back to my bed, hid under my covers, and cried myself to sleep.

Many have asked if I had been a victim of physical abuse from my father. Having reflected on this question many times, I can honestly say I do not believe I was. Sure, I received my fair share of "butt whoopings" while I was growing up, but I never remember being beaten by my father. There had been plenty of verbal abuse, but physical abuse I would deny. Either this is the truth, or I have suppressed such memories. My father seemed to have more restraint when it came to his children.

My mother never left my father; she continued to take the abuse until I became old enough to step in. As I became older, specifically as a teenager, when my father would start to go after my mother, I would place my body in front of him. There were several occasions when I would be thrown up against the wall and think this time was going to hurt, but it ended there. The anger in his eyes would defuse, and I would notice my feet returning to the ground. He never pushed it further than that, although he could have done major damage if he'd wanted to. I was never a match for him.

My childhood was not unique because of domestic violence alone. I began to realize there was a bigger, more dangerous problem in my family. I never thought much of all the "friends" my parents would have come over to our apartment. I started to recognize a pattern, however. People would come to visit, but their stays would be brief. They would arrive and follow my parents into their bedroom. After a short time, my parents and their guests would return, but they would be sleepy, as their eyes struggled to remain open.

The scary times were when their guests did not come out on their own. I would witness my parents in a frenzy, dragging a man or woman into the bathroom and placing him or her, fully clothed, into the bathtub. The cold water from the shower had little effect. My mother or father would slap the person across the face violently. I did not know it at the time, but these individuals came close to losing their lives due to heroin overdoses. Not everyone was saved.

There were many odd behaviors I noticed from my parents. Did all fathers fall asleep midday on their knees in the middle of the living room? Did all mothers fall asleep in a chair, attempting to scratch their face but missing altogether? Why did we routinely drive two hours each way from Bristol, Connecticut, to New York City? All we ever did was drive into the city, meet some random guy, then turn around and drive home.

One day I attempted to find out. Driving home, my parents pulled the car to the side of the road. As usual, I was told to play and not look up front. My eight-year-old mind was baffled by what I witnessed when I disobeyed and peeked into the front seat. Why was my dad tying a shoelace around his arm? Why was my mother holding the flame of a lighter to the bottom of a spoon as a strange liquid boiled in it? Why did my father stick a big needle into his arm? I am not sure when I learned the answers to these questions. It took even longer for me to understand my parents' addiction to heroin would be the root of all evil in our family.

During my early childhood, I was not aware of the impact my parents' disease had on our family. I was a typical boy, who enjoyed playing anything that involved a ball. I cherished the occasions my father and I would throw a football around, but even those times were not stress-free. My father held the belief that if the ball touched my hand, I should catch it. It did not matter how hard the ball was thrown or how much my body had to contort to reach it; I should not drop it. My father had a gun for an arm, and he did not hold back. There were times when I would have bruises on my chest and inner arms from the tip of the ball striking my body. I feared dropping any pass that got close to me. My fear was not because I believed I would get into trouble but because I longed for my father's approval and wanted to make him proud.

I became proficient at catching and throwing a football. My education on the latter, however, is not my recommended approach. My father had a group of male friends over one day, and they were all smoking marijuana (the least of my parents' addictions).

My father got me mad, and I threw something at him in anger. I was told I threw like a girl.

Everyone started to laugh at me. My father decided it was time to teach me how to throw "like a man." He went into his bedroom and returned with one of my mother's bras, which found its way into my hand. I had to throw it across the room until I did it "correctly." The laughter in the room heightened my anger, which increased the velocity of every throw. It had to have been one of the most humiliating moments in my first seven years of life.

Despite my lessons in manhood, my life seemed normal to me. I thought every school-age child went to the bar with his father on a regular basis. While at the bar, I never objected when my father would make me drop to the floor and do fifty push-ups in front of whoever would watch. Don't get me wrong—I did not like having to do them, but it made him proud, so I did them. I probably did more push-ups before the age of ten than many people do in their lifetime.

There was one positive I can remember from it all. When I was in fourth grade, my elementary school had its annual field day. One of the competitions was a push-up contest. I had to do more than seventy push-ups to take the lead. There were several kids to go after me, and I wanted to win this event. I was confident I could beat the seventy mark, but how many could the others after me do? I set my goal at one hundred. One hundred push-ups later, I had won the contest. I successfully defended my title for the following two years. Thanks, Dad!

On May 6, 1981, Nicole Francesca Ramirez was born, effectively abridging my childhood at eight years of age. It began innocently enough. Wanting to be helpful, I would change a diaper or two. Soon my responsibilities increased exponentially. I was left home alone with an infant for hours at a time as my parents' addiction began to take over their lives. Financial troubles, conflict with the law, and failed attempts at drug rehabilitation all had impaired their ability to provide parental care to my sister and me.

One day my sister and I were home alone in our two-bedroom fourth-floor apartment. I was a bored nine-year-old boy whose entertainment was playing with his infant sibling. I grabbed a book of matches, which were abundant in our house, given my parents' smoking habit. I started lighting matches one by one as I encouraged my thirteen-month-old sister to blow them out. It was a fun game. She was smiling and giggling, so we must have been doing nothing wrong.

Fortunately, a friend of my parents came over to the apartment looking for them. The back door from the kitchen was wide open that day, as we had no air conditioning, and it was a hot day. The friend walked up and saw us playing with fire. He ran into the kitchen, grabbed the matches out of my hand, and said he was going to tell my parents. For some reason, this did not scare me. I never got into trouble for my dangerous actions. How were my parents going to teach me about responsibility? I was not the one who left a nine-year-old with a one-year-old child.

The announcement of a third pregnancy was unexpected and confusing to my mother, who insisted she was faithful in taking her birth-control pills. What it meant to me was more responsibility. I had just survived my first sister's infancy. Now it was about to start over again.

At the age of thirteen years, I was not knowledgeable about infantile colic; I just knew my second sister was a handful. What I remember most were the sleepless nights. It would start in the early hours of the morning with a high-pitched cry. My mother would try her best to appease her newest daughter, but patience was not my mom's best quality at 2:00 a.m. Instead, I would be startled by my bedroom door being flung open and my mother screaming at me to get my sister to sleep. I would watch with barely open eyes as my infuriated mother stormed out of the room, leaving me to wonder what to do with my inconsolable sister.

This routine occurred nightly until I started keeping my sister in my bedroom from the beginning of the night. When she would wake up, I would try anything to get her back to sleep. I would feed her, rock her, pace the room with her; it did not matter. This child was going to cry until she decided to stop crying. She would cry so much that I would cry because I was so tired and hated doing this night after night. It took several months, but at the age of six months, she got over her colicky nature, returning peace to my life—well, at least at night.

Attending school during the day offered me a break from providing childcare, but even school was stressful for me. As crazy as things were at home, it was my haven. School was intimidating. Never owning a home, we occupied various apartments for short periods, and we got evicted often for failure to pay rent.

The frequent moving often placed me into a new school district, making me the dreaded "new kid" in school. Most of the time I was an outsider, often being bullied. As a result, I never made friends in school. I would go quietly to class, do what the teachers asked, and then take the bus home, where I felt most comfortable. At home, I felt I had a purpose and was needed, and this made me feel good.

EXODUS FROM CONNECTICUT

The summer of 1987 started like any other time for us. We were living in my grandmother's basement, battling the financial struggles that had become the norm for our family. I was about to start high school in the fall, yet had no feelings of excitement. I did not have any direction or focus on schooling at that time. Perhaps that was a blessing, because I would have been terribly disappointed if I had.

It was late one August evening when my mother came to me. She pulled me aside while we were in the basement and told me to start packing my clothes and anything else I thought I wanted—not that I had that much anyway. She explained to me that we were going to leave in the morning. Leave? For where? Another apartment? No, this time was different. My father had been involved in a minor motor-vehicle hit-and-run, and the police were looking for him. It was time for a major change—or an escape, to say the least.

In the early hours of the morning, before the sun rose, my parents, two younger sisters, and I packed all of our belongings into the back of our old Ford Pinto and left my grandmother's house with nothing but a note to my grandmother from my mother—no good-byes, no hugs, just a piece of paper expressing emotions of failure and hopes of a better life. I was confused and scared. We had just left everything we had. Even if it wasn't much, we still had family.

Where were we going? On the road, my parents shared what they thought was a plan that would change our lives for the better. My mother had a sister in Orlando, Florida. We were going to move down to Florida as well. How could we do that when we could not even stay in my grandmother's basement? Was my aunt going to take us? Knowing her, I didn't see that happening. So exactly what was this plan, and how was it going to happen?

Before I could process the thoughts further, my mother turned around from the passenger seat, opened an envelope, and examined the look of surprise on my face as I stared at the bills the envelope contained. She shared with me that $3,400 was in the envelope. I am not too sure how much that seemed like in 1987, but my parents were happy with it and felt it was plenty to help us start over.

The natural question I had was, How did a family that could not keep a roof over its head, that missed meals because its food stamps ran out, get that much money suddenly? Did our sudden departure have something to do with this newfound fortune?

I didn't have to ask; I knew the answer. At the time, my mother was working as a bookkeeper at a local accounting firm. My mother was one of the smartest people I have ever known. She may not have had degrees or many initials after her name, but she was intelligent. I do not know how she did it and never really wanted to know, but somehow, she embezzled the money from the firm. As I learned about the embezzlement, all I could think was, *Drive faster, Dad; drive faster.* Now not only was my father sought after by the police but my mother might be too. Did the accounting firm know yet?

The madness was all too much. I wanted to get away too. Florida could not get here soon enough. After all, who wouldn't want to move to Disney World? There was also the fact that my favorite cousin lived in Orlando. That was going to be great! Little did I know how long the drive from Connecticut to Orlando, Florida, would be. For a typical family, it is not too bad, maybe twenty-four hours, a straight shot down I-95. If you have not already picked up on the hints yet, we were not your typical family.

It was not long until it became obvious that this was not going to be a simple trip. New York City was only two hours from Bristol, Connecticut. It was there that my parents gave up any hope of starting over as a family in another state. New York City was my father's hometown. It was not that he had family or friends there but rather that he knew where to go to get as much heroin as he wanted or could afford. What I learned was that $3,000 could get you four days of good heroin and a sense of euphoria that grasped on to my parents so tightly that they could not escape. I wondered each passing day why we were not back on the road traveling to our destination. I am not sure I understood then that their addiction had paralyzed them.

By the time we left New York City, our financial situation suddenly did not look so comforting. It was by the time we got to Baltimore, Maryland, that I got the impression we were broke once again. Somehow we made it Fayetteville, North Carolina, before everything fell apart, and my parents' addiction compromised our safety.

I remember most of the events as if they happened yesterday. My mother was driving our old red

Ford Pinto that needed to be started with a screwdriver, as the ignition no longer worked (I never asked why). Most times it would not start at all, so my father and I had the rewarding task of pushing it from the rear as my mother popped the clutch. That was at least a once-a-day event.

So far the day was uneventful, and I was glad that I had not yet gotten into my exercise routine. My mother was in the driver's seat, my father in the passenger seat, and my two sisters and I were in the backseat. We did what we did every day, it seemed. Find the scariest, most dangerous neighborhood, and invite some stranger to approach the car. I suppose you just know who is a drug dealer. My parents sure did, as I can never remember them being wrong. The man who approached on this particular day did not seem any different from the rest. He bent over, peered into the rear seat, and spotted three young children. He continued to discuss business with my father.

The problem was that he did not deal in heroin. He was a cocaine dealer, but, of course, he knew where to get some good heroin. Desperate at this point, my parents let him into the car, where he sat next to me. The uncomfortable feelings were mutual, as I was trying to shield my sisters from him. A few blocks from where we met him, he got out of the car and told my father to give him the money, and he would get the heroin. My father wanted to go with him, but the man said that was not possible.

It was starting to get uncomfortable now, and the tension seemed to rise. My father then demanded to hold on to a few bags of the dealer's cocaine as collateral. The dealer was reluctant, but he sensed my father was not giving him any money until this happened. My parents lied to the dealer that they were not cocaine users and told the dealer there was no risk to them holding it. Eventually, the transaction concluded, and the dealer went off around a large brick building, never to be seen again.

I do not remember how long my parents waited before realizing that they had just been scammed, but let me just say they were less than happy. They'd just given what money they had for a heroin high, and what they got were four bags of drugs they did not use. Or did they? My father opened the small aluminum foil wrapping to see a white powder. Using the tip of his pinky finger moistened by his mouth, he dipped into the white powder. I am not sure how or even if he knew what cocaine was supposed to taste like, but whatever it was, it was not cocaine.

My father was never one to have control of his temper, and twice burnt was more than enough to set him off. The next five to ten minutes would turn into the most frightening event of my young life.

My mother, using the old flat-head screwdriver, started our debilitated Ford Pinto with a mission at hand. Sitting in the backseat, I did not know what was about to happen, but I easily sensed that my parents were upset, strung out, and plotting revenge. The motive was far more than simple revenge, but they needed their drugs. They were hurting from the withdrawal, and they were determined to do whatever had to be done to get their next high. To do this, they were even willing to put their family in danger, and they did.

We drove through another neighborhood that looked like all the rest. The houses looked uninhabitable. People would be sitting on their porches or standing outside on their lawns with seemingly nothing to do. It was a sight I got used to seeing every day, no matter what city we were visiting. Then, as always, a man approached our car. This gentleman was a young man, not too intimidating, and he appeared friendly, given that he was a drug dealer. I sensed that he might have been new at his trade.

My father started the conversation as the man bent over the passenger window to peer inside, scoping out the inhabitants of the car. It was confirmed that this dealer had heroin, and they started to discuss prices. Why was this happening at all? It was my understanding that we had just lost all our money when the last dealer stole it.

I was confused but didn't give it much more thought. I just continued to observe the events as they transpired. Once the deal was agreed upon by both parties, my father then asked to taste a sample of the dealer's supply. The dealer was reluctant to do this, but my father explained how he recently had been burnt on a bad deal.

The dealer was hesitant but eventually conceded to my father's request. First, the dealer requested that my mother turn off the car as she still had it running. This request imparted a silence that seemed to last forever. I watched my mother's right hand develop a slight tremor as it approached the ignition. The car was turned off.

I watched from behind the passenger's seat as my father opened a piece of tinfoil no bigger than a half dollar. Inside was a white powder that appeared to my untrained eyes to be the same as it always was. My father's fifth digit, moistened by a lick of his tongue, dabbed the substance and approached his tongue again The foil was carefully folded back up, securing the heroin that was apparently confirmed by my father. The tension started to build from that moment.

The dealer started to get uneasy and for a good reason. My father still had his drugs and had not shown any intention to pay. My father yelled, "Go!" to my mother. The screwdriver darted to the ignition, and my mother fumbled with starting the car. The dealer, realizing that my parents were attempting to steal his heroin, started to throw punches at my father through the passenger-side window. My father was defending himself from the seat with his fast hands, but one punch got through and landed square on his chin.

"Go!" Again, my father pleaded with my mother. The car stalled, and I thought this was the end. She got it restarted and slammed her foot on the gas pedal. As we peeled away, I let out a scream from the backseat. My father, frantic, asked if the dealer had hit me. I said no, as he had not, but even if I was hit, I surely wouldn't tell my father. Knowing him, he would have told my mother to turn the car around, and he would have gone after the dealer, which wouldn't have been brightest thing to do, since we'd just stolen drugs from him. He would have, though, for nothing would ever keep my father from protecting his family. He may not have been a prototypical father, and he surely did not spend much time playing games with us, but I never doubted his love for his children. He would have done anything for us, even if it put him in danger or even jail.

As we exited the neighborhood, I just remember tracking the dealer with my eyes, waiting for a gun to be pulled and aimed our way. Fortunately, that never happened. How different the events would have been if he had been in possession of a firearm. We were defenseless and at point-blank range. I relived that day many times in my dreams as a youngster.

That moment made me realize how bad a disease my parents had and how hard it was for them to battle it.

As the saying goes, we won that battle, but the war was not over. The next memorable moments came in Fayetteville, North Carolina. Needless to say, my parents' high from their latest dose of heroin did not last long, and we had no more money for anything, including food or shelter. How were we surviving? Where was the little food we consumed coming from, or how were my parents putting gas in our car, allowing us to progress down the East Coast, even if at a slow pace?

The answer is a lesson in panhandling that I learned by close observation of my mother's masterful skill. She could convince anyone of any story she wanted that person to believe. Be it on the streets or along rest areas on Interstate 95; my mother was convincing. My father would also be active in approaching random strangers and giving a sad story of how his family needed help, but my mother was by far the more successful earner. I have often felt saddened when I think of the day-in, day-out nature of efforts. How humiliated they must have felt. My parents were proud people, but they obviously had to swallow their pride and beg for help from anyone who would listen to them. It was not an attractive sight, and some days were better than others, but somehow it accomplished its task of feeding us and getting my parents their next fix, so they tamed the beast called withdrawal.

Sometimes the money would come none too soon. Heroin withdrawal was taught minimally in medical school (as least to me), but I would have been happy to have learned about it only in medical school. Instead, my knowledge of withdrawal came from observation of the pain and suffering of my parents.

My mother's withdrawal always affected me the most, however. It hurt me to see her withdraw, as I knew I was never able to help her. I would see her curled up, knees drawn to her chest, writhing on the sofa or on the floor. She would have violent episodes of emesis (vomiting). She would run to the bathroom as her bowels took control of her day. The pains were the worse, though.

As a young child, I did not know what was wrong or even if my parents were going to survive. It always seemed to stop eventually, only to be replaced by a state of sleepiness that I did not understand. Be it my mother or father, it looked the same. Their heads would nod, their eyes would close, and they'd have a look of scorn on their faces. There was always the characteristic scratching of their faces too. It was a slow, inaccurate movement toward the face with a soft scratching motion. If I was ever in doubt about whether they had recently used heroin, this was the sign I watched for the most (granted, there was never any doubt about their mental state).

Although the panhandling produced enough money to buy drugs and fed us once a day, it was usually not enough to shelter us. As a result, our evenings were spent at random homeless shelters, and we were surrounded by strangers with their struggles. I will not make it sound better than it was: it was scary, dirty, and uncomfortable. It started to instill a sense of hopelessness in all of us. The nights we could not find a homeless shelter with room to fit us, we stayed in our car and slept as best we could.

Then one day while panhandling on the streets in Fayetteville, North Carolina, my mother received a gift she never expected. An elderly gentleman she had approached happened to be a pastor of a small local church. When I say small, I mean small. It was a church in the middle of nowhere, surrounded by trailers that were inhabited by family members. The total occupancy of the church could not have been more than a hundred, but I doubt there were ever more than fifty people in attendance.

The pastor did not offer my mother money that day, but rather a place to live. There was a small living space in the back of the church that was offered to us as shelter. The pastor said we could stay there with only two stipulations: that my parents try to find work and that we attend the church. The desire to work was never really a limiting factor for my parents. Going to church, however, was asking for a miracle.

My mother did find work at a Waffle House waiting tables, and I believe my father worked on the construction of a new church. Unfortunately, our new home did not last long. After a month and a half, my parents failed to attend any church activities, and I'm sure they were still battling their addiction. The pastor, feeling that my parents were not trying to satisfy the stipulations set forth in the beginning, told my parents that we had to leave the church and move on.

I cannot say that I liked living at the church. They studied a religion that I'd never heard of, but the services were unique, as they often spoke unintelligible languages. Their culture was different, and I'm not sure we would have ever fit in, but I liked it better than our car or the cold, hard floors of the homeless shelters. It did not matter, though, how much or little I liked it there. More homeless nights were in my immediate future, and there was nothing I or anyone else could do about it.

Once again, we packed all our belongings into the back of our Ford Pinto, this time with one extra passenger onboard. While staying in the back of the church with no privacy, my mother had found a way to become pregnant once again. It was early in the pregnancy, but I am sure that this was nothing more than added stress for my parents. It had never been a consideration to abort the pregnancy. Even if money were not an issue, this was just something my parents could not and would not do. I know this because I asked them one day. They admitted having more children was a challenge, but no matter what the circumstances were, they would never give up their children, and they never regretted their decisions. All of us in our own ways brought love and happiness to their dark lives.

If not for us, my parents might not have survived. We were their reason for fighting to make it to another day. My mother often said she had thought about ending it all herself, but then she would look at her children and realize she still had a purpose in life. She may not have been doing the best compared to others, but she was doing the best that she could, and that was enough for us. Through it all, I sincerely believe we were loved deeply.

It took about three weeks to arrive in Orlando, Florida, from Fayetteville, North Carolina: homeless shelters by night, rest areas along I-95 by day. I was stuck in the back of the car, trying my best to keep myself and my two sisters entertained. There are so many details that I just don't remember them all. How did we eat? I learned about soup kitchens firsthand. I learned that many churches reached out to the community through their charity efforts. I watched my mother beg for money, using stories that would make any grown man cry. Even my father swallowed his tremendous pride and became an expert at panhandling. Somehow, it was enough to provide us with nourishment, gas for the car, and, of course, my parents' daily heroin needs.

When we arrived in Orlando, Florida, we visited with my mother's sister and her family. We were allowed to stay with them, but for a short time only. They lived in a small apartment complex and barely had room for themselves. Having an additional family of five invade their space was asking a bit much. We were forced back into a downtown homeless shelter. This one was different in that it had separate back living quarters for families. We were picked to stay there, which was a blessing because it felt much safer than in the auditorium-sized room with hundreds of homeless people who were mostly men. Compared to where we had been staying and what we had been doing during the day, this was great. My parents were still out hustling for money, but the kids got to stay with my aunt during this time.

I loved it because my favorite cousin was here, and we were reunited. We did almost everything together growing up. Not all of it was good, I hate to say. Growing up in poverty is difficult for anyone and is especially hard on children. It is difficult seeing other children with material things you don't have. You see them wearing the latest fashions when you are wearing secondhand clothes. It does not help when you are wearing a winter coat with someone else's name embroidered on it. I now realized as an adult that my parents did what they had to do to keep me in clothes, and, in this instance, warm, but I still to this day remember the verbal abuse I received in the school yard the first day I wore a winter coat with the name Benjamin on the front.

This led my cousin and me to engage in illegal activity starting at the age of eleven. Winters in Connecticut are very cold, and the winter coats are big and fluffy. They could hide numerous candy bars if one chose to do so. On many occasions, my cousin and I did just that. We would go to the local grocery store hungry, and of course, two eleven-year-old boys are not going to think about stealing meat and potatoes. No, we would head straight for the cookie and candy aisle. One time we stole a jar of pickles and olives and ate the entire contents in the woods.

The irony of this story is that it all came to a stop, albeit temporarily, when my cousin was ill with a head cold. I was not with him that particular day, but he had a sore throat and runny nose. We would stuff all kinds of items down our coats, and nobody knew as we walked out the front door of the store. On that day, however, he simply wanted to treat his cold symptoms, so he attempted to steal a pack of Halls. Somehow, he was caught, and that was the last time we "feasted" on our earnings.

My cousin and his family had moved to Orlando several months earlier. It was very hard for me having lost my best friend, even if for a short while. It was Halloween 1987, and on this night we did not have to steal our candy; we were going to trick-or-treat the night away! Some may say at thirteen years old, I was too old to go trick-or-treating, but I would argue that I deserved it. Indeed, it was a great night; I had finished the night collecting half a pillowcase of candy, and I was enjoying the fun that all young boys should have in life. I went to sleep that night happier than I had been in months. I wished that moment could last forever. Not only did it not last forever, but the morning brought on a whole new scare of its own.

My aunt had moved into their apartment just months earlier, but they still did not have furniture in the children's bedrooms. They complained about sleeping on the floor, and I do understand completely, but at that moment in my life, I was happy to have a carpeted floor and a pillow to lay my head on. We went to sleep that night on the floor, each of us with our pillowcases of candy by our sides. I remember waking up in the middle of the night to go to the bathroom.

There was a problem, though. I was having a difficult time getting up off the floor. All my joints were stiff and hard to move. I was not sure what was wrong, but after a few minutes, I could hobble to the bathroom, where I voided. I was afraid to lie back down on the floor, as I feared not being able to get up again. I walked into the living room and sat in the recliner, where I fell back asleep.

It was several hours later when I awoke. I thought I had had a bad dream where I hurt all over and could not move. Reality reminded me that it was not a dream at all. I attempted to rise from the recliner but could not. My large joints—my shoulders, elbows, hips, knees—all felt stiff and painful. I couldn't move from the recliner. I did not know what to do. Moments later, my cousins and our parents entered the living room. I told them I could not move. I looked well, and thus the family thought I was joking. My father, soon followed by my cousins, threw a piece of Halloween candy at me. I did not reach out to catch it; I couldn't.

At first, it was comical, and numerous pieces of candy struck me in the chest. However, they soon realized I was not playing a game; I truly could not move. I saw the expressions of laughter disappear from my parents' faces to be replaced by fear. My father picked me up into his arms and rushed me down to the car, hoping it would start and that we did not have to push-start our standard Ford Pinto.

What would he do? I was his wingman when it came to jump-starting the car. As fortune would have it, the car started on its own as soon as my mother put the screwdriver into the broken ignition. To this day, I still do not know why we had to start the car with a screwdriver, nor have I ever seen another car started in such a manner.

My parents sped downtown to the Orlando Regional Medical Center emergency room. I do not remember much of the first several days there. I know I spent five days as an inpatient, but I was well medicated; when I did start having memories of the hospital stay, it was a few days later. I remember a team of doctors surrounding my bed and asking all kinds of questions. Many, I felt, had nothing to do with what bothered me. Little did I know that one day that would be me leading a team of young doctors at the bedside of a patient, asking numerous questions while my patient contemplated his or her purpose.

I was diagnosed with rheumatic fever upon discharge. Rheumatic fever is an autoimmune response to Streptococcus bacteria, such as the bacteria that cause strep throat. The body's immune system attacks tissues in the body, such as the heart valves, that mimic components of the Streptococcus bacteria. I had sustained minor regurgitation of all four of my heart valves. In other words, they were all leaking blood backward. I was told I could do no strenuous activity for six months and had to take aspirin and penicillin three times a day until I was thirty years old. At fourteen, not being able to play basketball for six months seemed like an eternity, never mind taking pills three times a day until I was thirty!

I was not exactly compliant with the no-strenuous-activity part. I would come home all sweaty, and my mother would yell at me. "Were you playing basketball again? You know you can't do that."

"No, Mom. It was just hot out, and I was watching the other guys playing."

I'm sure she never believed me, but how does a parent regulate this part of a boy being a boy, and what does a fourteen-year-old know about the medical consequences of noncompliance? Fortunately, I never had any long-lasting issues from my episode of rheumatic fever. My last echocardiogram looking at the heart valves was normal, and I have led a fully active lifestyle ever since.

During my stay in the hospital, life as my family knew it continued. My parents were hard at work at a rest stop along I-4, the interstate that traverses Florida from Daytona to Tampa. I do not remember my parents visiting in the hospital, but in fairness, I was made pretty comfortable, and I like to think they knew it too.

I do know their nights continued at a homeless shelter in downtown Orlando. This is where I would join them upon my discharge from the hospital. Being a family, we stayed in the family section. Of all the shelters, this had to be the most family friendly. We were in a back room, fully separated from the other homeless, predominately single men. The family room had a television, and its entrance was run by a man named Dick; I do not recall his last name, despite his becoming a good friend of my mother. In fact, I can recall many holidays when Dick joined our family for dinner.

Dick, an older man who was overweight and a chain smoker, always seemed like a genuinely nice man, even if I found his relentless cough (which I now recognize as the cough of chronic bronchitis) annoying. I never got to know Dick much; then again, as a young teenage boy with no confidence, I did not get to know anybody. I believe his heart was in the right place, and somehow, I feel he helped us in ways I may never have known. Why else would my mother have become such good friends with this stranger?

So here I was, a fourteen-year-old boy confined by space. I spent every day in that family room with my sisters, as my parents were out trying to earn money. Every six hours I took my penicillin and my aspirin. Six months of no activity felt like an eternity too. I was told I had to take the penicillin until I was thirty years old—that was forever to me. I was going to be old and gray by the time I could stop taking medication. For now, I just wanted to play basketball and live whatever kind of normal life I could consider under the circumstances.

A month passed while we lived in the shelter. It never was a consideration to me that I should have started my freshman year of high school. It was now November; the school year was nearly half over. My parents could not enroll my sister or me into the public-school system without a place of residence, however. Can't say I was rushing to get back to school, however. I found nothing fun about school. I had become an introvert, and with relocating from school to school, I failed to make friends. In the homeless shelter, nobody was there to bully me.

My family had never been a religious family. My father had grown up attending Catholic schools, but we never went to a church of any kind with my parents. It was a Baptist church that arguably changed the course of my family's life, at least for a while, and for some of us longer than others.

It was nearly the holiday season, and the church youth group had adopted a family for the holiday season. That family was my family. Before I knew it, we were out of the homeless shelter and living in a house provided by the church. My parents were found jobs, and the only price they had to pay was to allow a woman by the name of Mrs. H to take my sisters and me to Sunday school and church. The agreement was that we could stay in the home for a year, and after that time we would have to find a residence of our own. My parents were encouraged to attend church as well, but they never did. My mother began working as a dispatcher for an electric company, and my father worked for the same company as a custodian. Now with a residence, my sister and I were enrolled in school. Nicole started kindergarten, and I enrolled as a freshman at Edgewater High School.

IF YOU CAN DO IT, I CAN DO IT BETTER

It was the beginning of December 1987, three weeks before the end of the first semester, and the students were preparing for semester finals. I do not recall what courses I took, but I remember there were only three I could start that late in the semester; the last four were study halls. I remember one of the classes was a year-long vocabulary course. I was told I had to take and pass the semester finals to get credit for the classes. I wish I could remember what my reaction was, but I do not recall getting too upset or thinking it was an impossible task. After all, I had three full weeks to prepare, and it wasn't like I could do anything physical. I was still imprisoned from my rheumatic fever.

So what if all the other students had three months to prepare? To me, it was the first sign of my competitive nature that would ultimately be my driving force for success. Somehow, I knew it would be hard, if not impossible, to pass these three exams, given that I had not been present for classes, but that was exactly why I was going to pass them. Indeed, I did pass all three exams, preventing me from having to extend my high school career before it even started.

My sophomore year of high school began at a new school, as we had to move out of the home we had spent a year in. This time I tried briefly to be more social. I joined the JV football team, but after three practices, one face mask, one tackle, zero games, and zero respect from teammates or coaches, I quit the team. I told the coach I had a heart issue, and my doctor had prohibited me from playing. This was not the truth, of course, as I had been cleared to participate in physical activity again, but I felt out of place and did not feel motivated to continue.

The academic year went by with me making one friend, and that friendship did not last long. I was content to just stay at home and care for my sisters. It had gotten to be the norm for my life. In fact, I felt it easier to care for three young siblings than to go to school or engage in any social activities. I did not see the purpose of attending school, and my grades showed it. I was a consistent C student during my sophomore year. I knew what I had to do to pass, and that was about all I did. I passed the time, ever so eager for adulthood so that I could leave my home and find freedom.

My junior year of high school I transferred back to the high school I started at as a freshman. If nothing else, my parents were getting consistent in yearly evictions from our place of residence. The year started as the two prior. I did not care about school or anyone there. I felt like I spent my life in two separate prisons: school during the day and home caring for my sisters during the evening.

I was now of a legal age to work, so I got my first job, working at a fast-food restaurant. My parents didn't want me to work initially, as that meant losing their evening help with the children, but it did not take long for them to accept my working when I handed over my paycheck. I did not mind, though. I did not work for the money, so I gladly handed over my paychecks to them. I knew we needed the money as a family, and I sincerely wanted to help out, but more than that, work was my escape from it all. I went in and truly enjoyed work. I strived to be the best at my job, and for the first time, started realizing the benefits of competition. I soon became a regular "employee of the month." Reflecting on it, I realized that this was the drive I needed to succeed. Some have called it an unhealthy drive, but in the end, it was what I needed to achieve the success that I have had.

As a child, I felt I never received any praise or encouragement from my family—that is my perception, of course. But for the first time in my young life, I felt needed and had a purpose at work. This newfound feeling of self-worth soon permeated my studies. I recognized that students who did well in school were getting recognition, and I wanted that too.

I remember the course that changed my attitude toward education completely. It was my junior general chemistry course. It was a challenging course, and not many did well in it. Those who did were known for their intelligence and adored by the teachers. I saw these students as competition. Who were they? Why were they special, and who said they were better than me?

This was the mentality I developed, the mentality that drove me to go home from school, work four-to-six hours, then come home and hit the books with an intensity and drive I'd never had before. Soon I was scoring the highest on tests in my chemistry class, and the student who was unknown, even to the teacher, was now at the top of the class. From there I wanted to be the best in every class I took. I was not always successful, but the days of getting all Cs were gone; I had become an A student. The taste of success was new to me, and my appetite for more grew strong. My senior year saw me for the first time in AP classes with the smartest students in my class, yet I had developed no fear. I held my own with them and was at the top of my AP biology class. Through it all, I don't remember my parents responding at all to my success. I believe they never knew of my struggles, and I never shared with them my dramatic turnaround.

College was in my sights, but where to go and how I was going to pay for it were challenges I had to suffer through on my own. I'm sure I had school advisers but never knew who they were, and there was not much guidance from my parents. Most students growing up in Orlando in the 1980s went to either Florida State University or the University of Florida. I had become a Florida Gators fan and sought to attend the University of Florida. I applied to the University of Central Florida in Orlando as well. In part due to an acquired cockiness and in part due to ignorance, I assumed I would be accepted anywhere I applied. Not everyone shared my confidence.

My family owes a lot to a wonderful woman I knew as Mrs. H. A part of my early success I credit to Mrs. H, but not in the way many believed. I recall a vivid conversation between Mrs. H and me about colleges and the financial burden that accompanies attending a four-year university. She told me I would not be able to go to the University of Florida, not because I could not get accepted, but because I would never be able to afford it. She stressed that I would have to apply to the local community college and hope to get a scholarship to attend.

I did receive a scholarship, but not to the community college that we discussed. I never applied there. Today I realized that it would have been a valid option, but at seventeen and with an ever-enlarging ego, I thought erroneously that going to a community college was a failure for me. I applied to the University of Central Florida first, not because I wanted to go there but because I felt pressured to attend. The University of Central Florida has developed into an outstanding university. At the time I was applying, it did not have the strong reputation it now enjoys. In my mind, I was a Gator, and nothing was stopping me from going to Gainesville.

The University of Central Florida was the first to reply: accepted. Along with the acceptance to their university was a full minority scholarship: a four-year education for free. Mrs. H was overcome with joy with the news, but I don't remember any reaction at all from my parents.

My reaction? I never accepted the offer; I had no intention of "settling" for the local university. In retrospect, I took an unadvised, life-altering gamble. In my early years, I blamed my ill-advised decision to decline UCF's acceptance offer before receiving an answer from the University of Florida on a lack of adult guidance, yet the truth remains that arrogance blinded me.

Fortunately, just weeks later I received an acceptance letter from the University of Florida, along with a full minority scholarship. I was going to be a Gator! I signed up for my dorm room and about packed my bags. What came next I never saw coming. Because I never had let anyone into my life, no one had ever influenced me.

During high school, I was not very popular. I kept to myself, a shy young man who lacked confidence. I ate lunch alone. It comes as no surprise, then, that I did not have any friends in high school; I just went, did what I had to do, and then went home. My senior year of high school started as the first three had. I had no desire to change anything or to get to know anyone. I had started to have success in the classroom, and I liked it. I saw the other students as my competition, and this made me work harder to be better than them—until my AP biology class, that is.

It was halfway through the year when I met my first girlfriend. As the final months of high school went by, our friendship grew stronger. It was a new personal experience for me, one that made me feel appreciated and loved. Soon my clarity about my future was clouded. She was an extremely bright student, graduating third in our class of 450 students. She got accepted to Emory University in Atlanta, Georgia. I had never heard of it.

It didn't matter. Once I realized that I was not going to convince her to go to the University of Florida with me, I did what any young teenager blinded by love would do: I canceled my dorm assignment at the University of Florida and declined the full scholarship they offered me. I was going to go to this Emory place; I was going to be with my girlfriend. What I did not know was that Emory is a competitive institution and that the deadline to apply had passed. Fortunately, their mother campus, Oxford College of Emory University, had an open enrollment. Oxford College campus was the original Emory campus. Located east of Atlanta, it was a two-year college with the junior and senior years completed on the main Atlanta campus. I was accepted, and with the generosity of the institution, I was granted near-complete financial aid to attend.

I needed 100 percent financial aid, however, as I had no assistance from family. A private institution, Emory charged nearly $25,000 for tuition; with room and board, the bill was even higher. As

I reviewed my financial-aid award letter, I was very happy to see how generous Oxford College was, but I was still $3,000 short, and nobody I knew had that kind of money.

Out of desperation, I reached out to someone I knew nothing about, someone whom I had not seen in many years: my father's mother. I wrote a letter to my grandmother, telling her how I'd been accepted to a prestigious college but needed some financial assistance to attend. Honestly, I wasn't even sure if she was financially able to help me, but my parents told me to try, as they thought she and her husband, an unknown stepgrandfather, lived a decent life.

I never received a response from my grandmother; my father was not surprised. She lived in New York City, but our family had no contact with her. I was visiting family in Connecticut, two hours from my grandmother, and decided to call my grandmother and see if we could meet up and talk about my situation. The phone conversation ended abruptly. I was told not to come to the city and that there was no need to talk. The dial tone from the corner payphone I used was the last sound I heard from my grandmother.

I returned to Florida having had a great visit with my mother's side of the family. My mother was one of seven children, and we were once all very close, spending many family picnics together. My mother's family was the polar opposite of my father's. My maternal grandmother practically raised me in my toddler years, yet they were socioeconomically deprived, and I knew I had no help to be found there. I returned to Florida with mixed emotions, happy to see family I missed, but disappointed by my interaction with my father's mother. The problem was I was upset and disappointed because I still lacked the resources to go to the college I wanted to go to, not because of how things went or ended with my grandmother.

My first true vision of religion was through the eyes of a Southern Baptist. My sisters and I were taken every Sunday to the Downtown Baptist Church of Orlando. It was initially an uncomfortable scenario for me, as I was shy and did not know how to act around my peers; I felt extremely out of place when compared to the other teenagers there. It did not matter how uncomfortable I felt, however, as we had to go, and frankly, it was a small escape from home, so I looked forward to Sunday mornings. I never fully engaged in the youth group. I went on several youth-group trips and did an occasional social event, but for the most part, I stayed to myself.

The youth group always sat in the same section of the congregation, yet I rarely sat with them. Instead, Bible in hand, I sat with Mrs. H and took notes as the pastor gave his sermon. Reflecting back, I wonder if they thought of me as snobby, and that was why I didn't associate with them. The irony is I was envious of them and felt that I was not good enough to be in their circle. I perceived them all as having all the things I did not have, material and otherwise, such as stable home lives. Driving me home from church one afternoon, Mrs. H asked me if I thought they were better than me. My inner voice whispered yes, but in my attempt at being strong and confident in myself, I told her no.

Of all the Sundays attending church over four years in high school, my brightest moment was a Sunday when the church honored the graduating high-school seniors. With the congregation full, we marched into the church with "Pomp and Circumstance" emanating from the organ pipes. Dressed in my cap and gown, I was asked to lead the graduates down the aisle to the pulpit. To me, the honor stimulated my sympathetic nervous system, causing goose bumps throughout my body. It was a simple feat, but I had spent four years in the shadow of all the other children in the youth group—but not on this day. I was the first to stand before the congregation as we were asked to tell everyone where we were graduating from and what our plans were.

On this Sunday morning, I committed myself before the entire church congregation that I was going to the University of Florida with plans of majoring in biology and further pursuing a career in pathology, which meant I was going to have to go to medical school. I had no way of knowing it at the time, but this annual church ritual for its graduation seniors was life changing for me, not because of my ego-stroking chance to lead the seniors, but because of the person who entered my life on that day.

Dr. G was a pediatrician in the community. I had never met him before, and in fact never had heard of him. After all the seniors were done at the pulpit, we greeted the congregation. A middle-aged gentleman with a beard approached me and introduced himself. He was a doctor and was "impressed by me." He offered me a summer job doing some research for him before I headed off to college. It was a great blessing, and I accepted.

The research involved chart reviews to extract data in an attempt to find a correlation between neonatal outcomes and maternal drug use during pregnancy. I had never done research before, and though I did not admit it at the time, I felt way over my head. To this day, I believe I failed at my attempt to help Dr. G, yet he never complained or told me anything about my work. I wonder if he ever completed the study, knowing he would likely have had to redo all the work I did.

Some people who enter our lives become influential when we don't expect it. To say this about

Dr. G is an understatement. In just a couple short months we had many conversations and interactions that changed the course of my future.

It all started when I changed my mind on which college to attend. I had planned to go to the University of Florida, as I had announced to the entire church congregation just weeks earlier. I had received a late acceptance letter from Oxford College of Emory University in Georgia. I knew very little about the college or Emory University. The reason for my application: my girlfriend was going there. I threatened my future college education by chasing a romance. Fortunately, the education was great; the romance, not so much.

I walked into work one morning, and the disappointment must have been all over my face. He pulled me into his office and asked what was wrong. I told him how I was accepted to Oxford College and was given a large financial package but was still short, and now I could not attend. He asked me how much I was short. When I told him three thousand, he laughed.

"That's all? I think we can figure something out, Jason." Not only did Dr. G pay the $3,000 balance to the college, but when I got there and had no money for books, he spoke directly with the bookstore manager, and the next thing I knew the manager was telling me to get all the books and supplies I needed, that everything was taken care of. I almost cried—then again, knowing me, I probably did cry later.

The next year, as I started my sophomore year, I was starting to panic as tuition bills were anticipated. What if I owed more? What if Dr. G was not going to help again? The bill came, and the university again showed its generosity, this time even to a greater degree. They provided all but $300! I supposed at the time they had to charge me something. I told Dr. G, and as you could expect, he was very happy not to pay $3,000.

He was so happy that when he saw my car, he observed that the tires were bad and bought me four new tires, stating, "Hey, I just saved twenty-seven hundred dollars this year. I can do this for you."

As generous as Dr. G was with his money, the biggest gift I received from him was a book I found at my workspace one morning. I had never heard of the author or the book, but it was a gift from a man I owed so much to, so I knew I had to read it. The book—*Gifted Hands*, by Dr. Ben Carson—sits on my home bookshelf, now with Dr. Carson's autograph on the inside cover, as I had the honor of meeting him.

As I read *Gifted Hands*, it became clear why Dr. G wanted me to read this book. Dr. Carson was raised by a single parent, his mother, on the tough streets of Detroit. A victim of poverty, Dr. Carson beat the odds and become a world-renowned pediatric neurosurgeon. There were many similarities between Dr. Carson and me, along with many differences. I read with intense interest as a young boy with an anger issue used education and faith to better himself. I adopted the self-motivating belief that "if they can do it, I can do it better."

It can be argued whether this mentality was good for me. My college years at Emory University were rather lonely, undoubtedly because of my attitude. I had a me-against-the-world attitude, and I saw everyone around me as competition. All were searching to gain one of the few spots in medical school. The year I applied to medical school, there were quoted to be forty-five thousand applications yet only fifteen thousand medical-school spots. Simple math said that at least thirty thousand young men and women would be disappointed by letters denying them their dream.

I was fiercely intent on not being one of them. The sacrifice was that I did not make many friends while in college. I was not in a fraternity, did not go to parties, and did not hang out in downtown Atlanta. The unfortunate part was that it never bothered me; I felt I never needed anyone. The most social part of my college life was participating in intramural sports. Even here it was never because I had friends who I played with, but it was my athleticism that made me desirable. Once the league was over, so were the pseudobonds that were made.

Were there times of loneliness? Sure, I felt it some, but I was so determined not to let anything or anyone stand in the way of my goal that it never became a lasting thought. I do remember one Thanksgiving in my senior year of college that was particularly hard. I was not able to go home for the holiday, as I had no vehicle and could not afford to travel back to Florida. The campus, fortunately, stayed open, and so I was allowed to stay in my dormitory room for the break, but it seemed as if I was the only one who did. It seemed like the longest four days of my young life. There was virtually nobody on campus, and most things were closed. Needless to say, there was no turkey dinner that year. It was the first time I truly felt alone, and the first time it bothered me.

A month later I would not be alone for the Christmas holiday. I traveled home and spent Christmas Eve with my parents and siblings in Florida. Christmas day I had to fly to Philadelphia, however, as I had a medical-school interview the day after Christmas. I had been offered a handful of interviews. It was great having multiple interviews and the opportunity to potentially pick a school that was best for me, but it came at an expense.

Fortunately for me, I again had help in the process. I knew Mr. Parrish as an attorney in the church.

His son was in the church youth group, and we were the same age. Beyond that, I did not know about the huge heart that he possessed until I graduated from high school. When I went off to college, he and his wife expressed how proud they were of me. At the time, I did not realize the significance of their sincerity. When it came time to interview for medical schools, I needed a suit. I'd never had one, nor did I see how I was going to get it.

I do not remember exactly how it came about that the Parrishes came to my rescue, but I do remember the day I was getting fitted for a new suit. The Parrishes were watching every measurement, it seemed. One of the funniest quotes I recall coming from Mr. Parrish was during the fitting: "Jason, promise me that when you are a doctor and are making money, you will put some meat on that butt." I had to laugh, as I knew what they meant. I was five feet, eight inches tall yet only 130 pounds. Indeed, I was skinny, but food was a luxury in my youth, and up until then, I had not had the opportunity to enjoy the pleasures of abundance.

The night before my flight to Philadelphia, I put on my new suit and glanced in the mirror. I had never worn a real suit before. Although nerves were starting to creep in, I had a feeling about this interview at this medical school. I had never heard of the school and applied to it only because my roommate in my junior year recommended I apply there. He too was applying to medical schools and was researching the many schools along the East Coast. He told me about this one in Philadelphia that was known for recruiting women and minorities. I could apply to ten schools for free, so I added it to the list. I knew nothing more about the school or the city of Philadelphia, but as I departed the next day, I felt calm about this interview. This continued the day of the interview. The day was very laid back and stress free, perhaps because it was the day after Christmas, but I chose to take it as a sign of a warm, welcoming school.

I was escorted to my interview by a medical student after a morning of orientation. I entered the office of a doctor in the Department of Emergency Medicine. He was in jeans and had wire-rimmed glasses and a ponytail. He welcomed me and said that he had not had a chance to review my file yet and asked if it were okay if he took a minute to read the personal statement I had written as part of my medical-school application. I told him that would be fine, and as he read, I sat back in my chair and felt a confidence flow over me. I had written about my family struggles, parental addiction, homelessness, and my motives for attending medical school. After he completed reading my statement, he put down the paper and just stared at me.

"What are you doing here?" he asked with a quizzical look on his face. I did not understand his question.

"Um, I'm applying to medical school," I replied.

"I know, but you should be one of three things, and sitting here at this interview is not one of them. You should be either strung out on the streets, in jail, or dead. You are here. How?"

I truly believe he was not ignorant by his questioning. I believed he was sincerely asking how I defied the fate that statistics said I should have followed. "Well, sir, I want to be a doctor. As far as I know, I have to go to medical school to do that, but if you know another way than attending four more years of school, please let me know!"

We both laughed at the honesty of my answer. One week later I received the letter I had been working so hard for:

"Congratulations, we would like to offer you acceptance to..." Although I still had interviews to other medical schools lined up, I canceled them all and accepted my offer to the Medical College of Pennsylvania—Hahnemann University School of Medicine. I felt I was being called there, and I had always followed my instinct. I am sure this made Mr. Parrish happy, as he had provided the financial means for my interviews, including travel and lodging. It is fair to say that I would not be a doctor today if it were not for the Parrishes.

DEPRESSION TAKES HOLD

My last semester at Emory University started great, with an acceptance letter to medical school; the dream was coming true. It was not to last long. On February 2, 1999, I received a phone call that my maternal grandmother had passed away while in the hospital. Unlike my relationship with my paternal grandmother, I was very close to my grandma Chase. She had been an amazing woman, raising seven children. All of them loved her, and I spent much of my early childhood years with her.

She had been in the hospital getting a procedure called a coronary angiogram. She had been having chest pains, and they were due to blockages in the arteries supplying blood to her heart. The doctors did the standard procedure of a heart catheterization and opened the blocked vessel with a balloon, called angioplasty. She appeared well afterward and was walking the hospital floor when she collapsed. She had what is called massive pulmonary embolus, a blood clot that went to the lung.

The phone call from my uncle initiated a pattern of depression that would plague me for years to come. I had never experienced the death of anyone I cared about before. After I hung up the phone with my uncle, I left my dormitory room and walked around campus for hours, seemingly lost, as multiple people I passed stopped and asked with concern if I were okay. The days and weeks that followed found me struggling to get out of bed. I slept for days, missed class regularly, and failed to eat.

My grades plummeted, and in fact, I was failing a couple of classes. Somehow, I found the strength and determination to buckle down, needing to ace my final few exams in several classes just to pass. I found the focus to study again and pulled several all-nighters. I passed all my classes and escaped a near disaster of not being able to go to medical school because I could not graduate from college.

My reward for the entire last-ditch effort was a graduation day where I sat by myself, surrounded by classmates who had large groups of family and friends supporting them. I mingled with one or two friends I had made, but mostly I just wanted to get my diploma and get out of there. It was embarrassing—and, I'll admit, hurtful—that I was without family at my college graduation.

Finally, I stood at the base of the stage awaiting my name. As my name was called, I walked across the stage proudly, fighting the sadness I felt inside. I did not want anyone to notice my pain. As I exited the stage, descending a short level of stairs, I was met at the bottom by a professor I had in my last semester. During the semester while I was struggling to pass her class, she reached out to me, feeling that something was wrong.

I had told her about my struggles during the semester and later told her how I felt about not having family coming to graduation. She made it a special point to be at the bottom of those stairs just for me. As I took my final step down, she greeted me with a smile, gave me a warm hug, and said, "I am so proud of you, Jason." For the moment, I didn't care that my family was not there. I hugged her back and thanked her. My sadness was vanquished by a woman I barely knew, yet her act of kindness was exactly what I needed, and somehow, she knew it. It was a moment I will never forget.

All the hard work, dedication, and sacrifice had paid off; I was starting medical school. In the summer of 1995, I found myself in a new city, the city of brotherly love, Philadelphia, Pennsylvania. I arrived via airplane late in the evening while darkness kept my new home a mystery. The next morning, I exited the building that the cab driver had dropped me off at the night prior. I walked one block, and as I turned the corner onto Broad Street, I froze with amazement, straining my neck as I looked up at arguably the most artistic building I had seen in my young life, a building with exquisite architectural detail located in the center of the city. Atop the building was a figure I later would learn was William Penn. My first sight of Philadelphia's city hall has always been one of my memories of the city.

I began my medical-school experience attending a six-week summer minority program. It consisted of an introduction to anatomy, physiology, and biochemistry, all courses taken in the first year of medical school. Grades during this six-week program did not count, but it served as a prep course in some ways. I used it more as an opportunity to get to know my new environment and a few classmates before the grueling work of the semester started. I at least accomplished one of these goals. I spent much of the six weeks walking around the city center of Philadelphia, enjoying the historic sites and the personalities of South Street. Before I knew it, the summer program was over, and though I become familiar with a few classmates, no long-lasting friendships were to be developed; as the academic school year started, I drifted away from those I took the program with.

The first two years of medical school are consumed with hours of classroom lectures and laboratory studies, not my style of learning. I was never one to sit in a large classroom and listen as a lecturer put slides on a large screen and mostly read them. It did not take long for me to stop going to class. The class notes were easily obtainable, as there were transcribed from audio recordings; textbooks were normal in the twentieth century, and I knew how to read. Most concepts in the medical sciences do not need much explanation, but rather an abundant amount of time to memorize concepts and an ability to understand mechanisms of body functions that later helped me analyze clinical scenarios of when those basic mechanisms failed. I felt I could do this on my own by reading the material myself.

Anatomy lab was vital to go to, but even here I fought the norm. I would not join my anatomy group during the day. With much disapproval from the group, I would go into the anatomy lab, a large room with an unmistakable aroma of formaldehyde and cadavers lined from one end of the room to the other, and turn off the main lights. Each dissecting table had an individual overhead light; under the illumination of the overhead light, I would listen to music through my headphones, embrace the company of no other living person, and become lost in the dissection of the cadaver. Though I thought the experience was great, it just epitomized the solitude that was my life, yet I did it to myself, not knowing or even believing that it was harmful.

For the most part, the first two years of medical school were without drama. I passed all my classes despite my lack of attendance, yet I do believe in retrospect that I would have done better and gotten more out of those years had I been more of a presence. Instead, I would live vampire hours, sleeping through the daylight hours and staying up most nights with my books and notes, committing them to memory. I would show up for the exams, pass them, and then the cycle would start again.

Why would I choose this lifestyle? Though there were a few of us who would be walking around the quiet halls of our medical school in the evening through the early morning hours, for the most part, I was by myself—just as I preferred it. There were about 250 students in my medical school class, and I knew the names of about 10 percent of them.

I did date in medical school, and it started almost immediately. By the end of the minority summer program, I had started dating a classmate whose origin was Jamaican. She was a former Ms. Teen Jamaica and had a happy personality. However, it was a short-lived relationship, lasting less than a year. I believe the stress of medical school led to an emotional disconnect.

The relationship broke down when I met a fellow medical student in the class ahead of me named Penny. The previous years of my life I was content with being alone and felt I didn't need anyone in my life to be happy. Penny and I connected the first day we met. I felt cared about, and despite what I had previously thought, I needed and wanted the attention, and I had not been getting that in my current relationship.

Penny and I dated for three years until my need for attention once again led to my seeking another relationship, though this time things started off a bit differently. Penny graduated a year ahead of me in medical school. She chose to do her medical training in the field of internal medicine at a program in New York City. I had hoped that she would stay in Philadelphia, but I did not want to pressure her or take her away from the training program she wanted to go to. I remember Penny using the phrase "out of sight, out of mind," and to some degree, I believe this is what happened to us.

Inside I was angry that Penny chose to go to New York for her training, though in all honesty, Philadelphia and NYC are not far away. Truth was, I was alone without her, she was a great friend, and she had showed unconditional love to me. When she left for training, I felt like I had lost my support system and my best friend. The void would be filled in an unusual manner, not by someone closer but rather farther away, by someone who taught me what passion and excitement were.

It had been a calm day in the internal-medicine service. I could study most of the afternoon, as there had been no admissions. I had been assigned to do a month of my internal-medicine clerkship at a hospital in New Jersey. I packed up my books and anticipated an early departure from the hospital's medical library when my pager went off, and the familiar number of my senior resident displayed across the screen.

I thought of not answering the pager and just going home, but this would be bad form. Logic prevailed and I answered, anticipating the page was to inform me of a new admission. I was not disappointed; we had an elderly man in the emergency room who was being admitted for chest pain, a man who would prolong my workday. I went down to the emergency room with my team of residents, assisted with the obligatory history and physical exam of our new patient, and then left the hospital for the evening.

The next morning, I was to see Mr. S, whom I had helped admit the evening before. Initially, when I got the page for the admission, I was disappointed, as I wanted to leave for the day, but as soon as I met Mr. S, any feelings of anger went away. He was quite the character, with a great sense of humor that made caring for him easy, and I was excited to come back to see him the next day. Little did I know that my excitement would soar to an indescribable level when I entered his hospital room.

Mr. S sat comfortably in a chair positioned against the wall to the left of the room's entrance. My attention, however, was instantly focused on the young woman sitting atop the windowsill several feet away from her grandfather. She sat with her arms by her side, her hands grasping the edge of the windowsill. She had a smile that illuminated the room and a cheerful voice that would improve anybody's bad mood instantly. I'm not sure that I even said hello to my patient initially; instead, I was drawn to the back of the room, where I approached Jersey girl.

Typically, I had always been a shy man who never made a first move, but the magnetic draw overwhelmed me. We instantly started up a conversation while seemingly ignoring the others in the room. It soon become apparent that there was going to be a major barrier to a relationship forming. She lived in Boston and was only in New Jersey because her grandmother was hospitalized for heart failure. Now her grandfather was admitted with chest pain, and she had spent the past twenty-four hours going from one hospital room to the next.

It just so happened she was in her grandfather's room at the time I did my daily rounds. An introduction in a patient room became an evening walk on the beach and a night sitting on the rocky jetty that once existed on the Jersey shore. The hours flew by as we began learning about each other. One little scoot closer became a gentle shoulder nudge, which turned into our first kiss.

Despite the distance, we spoke often on the telephone, listening as hours went by, laughing until our sides hurt. We tried the best we could to make a long-distance relationship work. Whether it was the distance or our dramatically different personalities—she was the artist, and I was the scientist—even our extreme level of passion was not enough. We both had suffered devastating losses in our lives, and not being near to console and support each other undoubtedly took its toll. She had lost her grandmother, a woman I had the honor to meet, though only for a short time. It took part of her soul, I believe, and there was nothing I could do to fill the void. From my perspective, this was the first time that the geographic distance we were battling was joined with an emotional distance.

As part of my attempt to regain the relationship and closeness we once shared, I chose to do my surgical residency in Boston, Massachusetts. I had hopes that this would be the answer and would make us grow as a couple. Two things happened that led to the end of those thoughts and ultimately to our relationship. A month before my medical-school graduation, my father ended his fight with end-stage liver disease, otherwise known as cirrhosis.

My father had been sick for the previous couple years as his liver began to fail. He had contracted hepatitis C from the years of heroin abuse and the common practice of intravenous needle sharing. My father also liked his beer; he was rarely ever seen without two cans in his hands. The combination of chronic hepatitis C and chronic alcohol abuse irreversibly damaged his liver, and he developed cirrhosis. He lost much weight, developed recurrent ascites (fluid that builds up in the abdomen), needing to have his abdomen drained of the fluid several times. There were also periods of aggression and confusion that are hallmarks of hepatic encephalopathy, a condition caused by ammonia buildup in the blood, when the liver fails at its job to excrete ammonia.

During the years my father's health was declining, I was immersed in my medical studies and went home to Florida only once or twice. To me, the decline seemed rapid, but I am sure for my sisters, who witnessed it all happen, it was a slow, painful decline. I was knowledgeable enough to know that my father was very sick but not skilled or knowledge-able enough to do anything helpful. In all fairness, there was nothing any medical provider could do at that time.

One afternoon while I was studying in my apartment in Philadelphia, my home phone rang. It was a funeral home in Florida, and they were calling me to ask some questions about the cremation for my father. When the woman on the phone realized that I had not been informed of my father's passing, I heard her voice change, and I felt sorry for her as I pictured the look of shock on her face. She apologized several times for being the one to inform me of my loss, and I knew it was sincere. I just never understood how it came to that. Why had my own mother not called me and told me that my father had died? Instead, a poor stranger, miles away, was burdened with surprising a young man with the news of his father's death.

My memory of the last month of medical school is minimal. I started sleeping days away, not knowing at the time that it was the beginning of a dramatic alteration in my career and life. Graduation day came, but there was a huge void in the day. My mother and two of my three sisters made it up from Florida to attend the ceremony, but the man I wanted to be there could not be. Shortly before his passing, my father sent me a handwritten letter, promising to be at my graduation:

Dear son, alias Dude, Dr. J,

Sorry I haven't written you sooner but I am sure you understand. I've been moved around like a piece of shit lately, but now I have an efficiency apartment and feel a lot better about life and everything else. I hope this letter finds you in the best of spirits and safe. I still can't get over you becoming a doctor in just three and a half months from now. You just don't know how proud I am of you. My son a doctor, wow. Sorry I didn't help or support you in your choice but I was tangled up in a fucked-up web of evil and drugs and to me that came first instead of you. Hope you understand, which I am sure you do by now. The bitch is that when we got all that money I knew we were in trouble but blocked it out like an asshole I can be most of the time. I discussed with your mother and Nicole about renting a car with our tax return and coming to your graduation by hook or crook we will be there I swear. It's gonna cost about $125 each to rent a car and gas to get there and another $75 for a couple of nights in a hotel room. I can't stay more than three days, sorry but we will be there rain, shine, snow or sleet. All you have to do is let your mother know the day you graduate. Well as you know I am not one for a lot of words in a letter because there is just too much to talk about. In person, you know I never run out of things to say. Hope this reaches you safely and will *see you on big G day. Love you as I always have but never showed it. That is because I have been an asshole all my life but I have changed and now I've learned to appreciate every day, one at a time. Be waiting to receive an answer from you, until then hit the books hard and kill 'em. Show 'em us Ricans are smart at times.*

Love you,
Your ever-loving dad
See you in May.
God bless you, son.

It meant everything to me to have had my parents at my medical-school graduation. I had gone through my college graduation without either of them, but this was it, no more graduations. The long, difficult journey to success was celebrated on this one day. Of course, I did not blame my father or feel angry that his presence was missing; I was just sad. What did anger me was a moment that should not have surprised me. During the latter stages of the ceremony, the parents of all the graduates were acknowledged and asked to stand for a warm applause. It was touching moment, one that I initially felt brought my father to the ceremony despite his lack of physical presence. Later when I was talking to my mother about the moment, I learned that she had missed it; she was outside smoking a cigarette. My level of disappointment was high when I heard my mother had missed that part of the ceremony.

I arrived in Boston in the summer of 1999, believing my life was just about to begin. My efforts during eight years of higher education had all been for this moment; I was to begin my surgical training. Just as important to me was that I was going to do it with the one I loved finally by my side. I had picked Boston as the place to train not solely because of the program, though the community program I was accepted to was my top choice, but for what I thought was the best chance to be together with my Jersey girl.

During our relationship, we had never lived in the same state, and during my fourth year of medical school, she was touring the country with a musical group. Most of the time I did not even know where in the country she was at any given time, nor was I able to communicate with her; smartphones did not exist, and long distance on a cell phone was not an option financially. On a rare occasion, I could use a prepaid phone card and get a sneak update on her life on tour, but that was not common.

When the tour ended, she went back to New Jersey with her mother. I was under the impression she would move with me to Boston; after all, that was my master plan. It did not happen for reasons

I have never understood. I was deeply troubled by this, and the combination of long work hours, grieving the loss of my father, and the failure of my only support system to be with me equated to failure. I had not known it at the time, but I was clinically depressed. I had minimal responsibility during the one month leading up to graduation and none until residency started, which made sleeping days away nothing more than what I thought was well-deserved rest. Once I started residency, the level of dysfunction my depression was causing became painfully apparent to all.

Residency training in medicine is a grueling time for any disciple, but for surgical trainees, it is especially difficult. I was in a small community program with only three residents per year, which meant I was on call every third day. Currently, resident work hours are restricted to no more than 80 hours a week. However, this restriction did not exist in 1999, nor could it be followed when I was working every third night. A typical workweek was easily 110–120 or more hours. The first month I worked through the transition, losing myself in the work and love for surgery I had. Soon, however, it became too much, and I started missing days of work. I would sleep through the workday, ignoring the ringing house phone, if I heard it at all. I stayed in bed, as I did not feel emotional pain while I slept. The result, however, was anxiety about going into work and facing the consequences of my absences, which led to more hiding in the form of hibernation in the safety of my bed.

I had been approached several times by my program director about my absences, and each time I had no explanation. They questioned me about drug use, which I quickly denied. I did not realize the true problem, was in denial that I was depressed, and failed in my last attempt to keep my job. I was told that if I missed one more day, I was going to lose my position in the training program. The anxiety won as I slept the day away again. My certified letter soon came in the mail. I had a choice: resign or have my contract terminated. I wrote my resignation letter and left Boston feeling like the past three months had been a year.

Without a job, I could not support myself in the expensive city, leading to my belongings going into storage and my life becoming myself and my car. My options were limited. I could go to Florida, where my mother and her new boyfriend had welcomed me, or I could go to New Jersey. I had become very close to Jersey girl's mother, Robin. I always felt comfortable talking to her, and in fact, I spoke to Robin more often than I ever had to Jersey girl.

It did not matter what I had to talk about; Robin was always there to listen to me. We would constantly laugh over the phone. One afternoon while I was still in Boston, Robin and I talked about what had happened to my position in the training program and that I had no place to live, as I could not afford my apartment anymore. She invited me to move in with her family, which now included Jersey girl. It was not exactly the plan I had for Jersey girl and me to be together, but it would be the first time we lived in the same area. Unfortunately, the circumstances and timing—and, more importantly, my psyche— were not ideal for our relationship.

I started working in the local mall to support myself. Talk about a hit to your ego: I had a medical degree, and I was working two jobs in the mall, one selling shoes, the other selling figurative candles at a mall kiosk. My depression got worse; I was angry and felt unsupported. It was all selfish on my part, although I only realized this years later. I was starving for attention, and though I had it right in front of me, I did not realize it. Jersey girl and I were finally together, and her family could not have been more supportive, yet I sought comfort somewhere else.

The first woman who showed me any attention drew me into an emotional web that damaged my relationship with Jersey girl and her family, and rightfully so. Long story short: do not get involved with a woman when you are living in the home of another.

I left New Jersey with no other option but to return to Florida; my mother allowed me to come down to stay with her in a small town on the Gulf coast called North Port. It was a town, unlike the big cities I had become accustomed to. My mother now was living with her boyfriend and my two youngest sisters. They had a small, three-bedroom house. I did not care; I was just happy not to be sleeping in my Honda Civic.

Living out of my car was a reality I had to face. Before I made the drive down to Florida from New Jersey, I was living in my car, as I had no other option. With the few belongings I had still in a storage unit in Boston, and my clothes and pride in the back of my Honda, I drove to my mother's home as I was taught years before, stopping at rest areas along the way to check in to my Hotel Honda, as I called it. I would take short naps at the rest areas then go back to driving. Despite watching my parents panhandle for money in the past, I did not have the courage to do it. I just drove on and finally reached the comfort of my mother's home once again.

During the five months I stayed in North Port, I held a few different jobs, realizing that I needed to earn my way as my mother and her boyfriend, although comfortable, could not afford to support me, nor was it their job to do so. It was surprising and discouraging to me to find that holding a medical degree did absolutely nothing to help me find employment; rather, it was a negative factor in some instances, making me "overqualified" for various jobs. I started at JC Penney selling shoes again. I also started working at a local restaurant for the breakfast shift, serving on a part-time basis. It was fun, as it was a small establishment attached to a motel. The motel serviced minor-league baseball players during a training session, which it was at the time. They would come to eat breakfast most mornings I worked, so I waited on many of them, though I never knew any of the players.

We would also get our regulars, who came to eat and socialize with friends. One particular morning still stands in my memory and makes me laugh. Most of our regulars were elders, who sat for hours drinking coffee and talking with friends. They were some of the best customers, and I got to know a few.

One morning two men were sitting in my section, and I overheard them talking about health and one of the gentlemen's health problems. He was talking about having heart failure and how it made him short of breath. His friend, who apparently did not have heart failure, was asking more about the heart failure and what it was and how he felt; the poor gentleman was trying his best to explain what he knew, but he was struggling. I then did what any good teacher would do when given the opportunity: I sat down next to the gentlemen, turning over the paper placemat on the table, and diagramed the heart and the process causing his symptoms of shortness of breath. Both men, at full attention, marveled, and when they finally looked up at me, their faces were masked with a puzzled look. "That makes so much sense," they said. "How do you know all this?" I simply responded that I read a lot and smiled as I handed them their breakfast check.

A SECOND CHANCE AT MEDICINE

I did attempt to gain a spot in a surgical residency again. I got a couple of interviews at programs that did not fill their allotted spots through the match, the system used by medical students and various programs to match students with their desired training programs. My history of leaving a previous training program made me a risk to any future programs.

I then had to search my soul to figure out what else in life I wanted to do. I was working two jobs, one as a waiter and the other as a barista at a bookstore coffee shop; neither would make me happy forever, nor would they pay back eight years of higher education. I remembered my family-medicine rotation in medical school and realized it was the opposite spectrum from surgery in every way, from personalities to job description. I had enjoyed the rotation as well, and besides my surgery rotations in medical school, family medicine was the clinical rotation in which I received the highest grade.

I researched programs that did not fill during their residency match for family medicine; they were numerous. I searched by location. I had heard about the family-medicine residency training program in York, Pennsylvania. It had a strong reputation as a top training program.

I found out that a classmate of mine had been an intern at York Hospital after we graduated. I called the program, and I talked over the phone to my former classmate, John, about the program, as well as the pros and cons of the area. I knew John from medical school, but I would not call him a close friend. We played basketball periodically, which made me nervous, as I was competitive on the basketball court, and most others did not like my court personality. John must have put in a good word for me; at least he did not speak poorly of me. I received an offer to join the training program at York Hospital in York, Pennsylvania, starting the summer of 2000.

As July 1, 2000, approached, I started to panic. Family medicine? What did I know about family medicine? I was the prototypical surgeon wannabe in medical school, god complex and all. I specifically remember teasing classmates who were interested in family medicine, giving comments like "I thought you wanted to be a doctor." I was so laser focused on surgery as a medical student that I spent my clinical years choosing all surgical electives, taking the minimally required rotations outside the field of surgery. I knew surgery fairly well for the level of training I had, but medicine, pediatrics, gynecology, and the many other disciplines that make up the clinical field of family medicine, were areas I felt I had minimal knowledge of. I never believed I would be using any of the skills or knowledge I learned about them in school, yet here I was, about to begin a three-year training program to become a family doctor. I soon realized that the breadth of knowledge in family medicine was far greater than the surgical field and the level of respect far less.

My return to Pennsylvania saw my return to medicine and also to Jersey girl. We talked sparingly during the months I was in Florida, but we decided that we would give our relationship one more try, hopefully with a fresh start in a new town. To me it was rather simple: I would find an apartment that we would live in and have a relationship like most people did who live in the same state. Emotionally I was doing better; I had a new start in medicine, and I was getting back together with someone I desperately wanted to be with. Finally, life was coming together well—so I thought.

Step one was getting an apartment, not an easy task when you are starting with no financial backing. I had started my job in the residency program, and it paid well enough to pay the bills, but to get started, I needed first and last months' rent, assets I did not have. For the first two months of my residency training at York Hospital, I lived out of my car, secretly sleeping in the hospital resident call room every night and getting my clothing from the car each day. I figured it was just a matter of time until I earned enough money to get an apartment.

One day my program director, the director of the residency program who was in charge of most things related to the program, called me into his office. He told me he heard I was sleeping in the call room, and that this was not acceptable. I explained that it was not my choosing, but I had nowhere to live. All my belongings were in my car, and although I could sleep in the parking lot each night, I thought the better option was the call room.

He expressed his understanding but insisted that I could not live out of the call room. He inquired about the reason I was staying in the hospital, and

I told of the financial barriers to getting an apartment. He asked what it would take to get an apartment and thus get me out of the call room. I told him I was looking for a place close to the hospital and was just waiting until I saved $800.

Without any hesitation, my program director, one of the kindest persons I have ever met, said simply, "Jason we can't have you living in the call room anymore. I will give you the eight hundred for the apartment fees, and you can pay it back as you can."

At first, I could not believe what I just heard; why would someone just give me $800? First, he gave me a job, a risk he took, given my surgical experience. Now he was giving me a personal monetary handout of significant value. Though I did not understand why he would do this for me, I had no other option, and so I graciously accepted, feeling both fortunate and embarrassed it had to come to this. I promised him I would pay him back over time; I had three years to do it, so I believed it would be easy to do. As we all know, however, nothing is guaranteed.

I moved into my apartment the next week. It was a one-bedroom, two-level apartment a couple of miles from the hospital. It did not have the bells and whistles of some apartment complexes, but it was not my car or the call room, so I embraced it. Jersey girl and I made a trip to Boston. I still had belongings in storage in Boston, and we loaded a U-Haul truck and together completed my move out of Boston. My plans were coming together so far. All that was left was to get my girlfriend to move in with me, and life would be perfect.

Several months passed, and I was still making trips to the Jersey shore, a three-hour drive, to visit Jersey girl. I never understood her reservation about moving, but it never happened.

Medical residencies start in July of each year. By the holiday season, I felt our relationship was starting to be strained again by distance. I wanted to be able to come home and be with the one I loved on a regular basis. I repeatedly told myself that it would be soon.

Christmas day was rapidly approaching, and I had a plan. We would have our first Christmas day by ourselves, together, in our apartment. I decorated a tree, put up mistletoe, and wrapped presents I thought she would thoroughly enjoy; it was going to be the beginning of many Christmas days to come. I made the drive to New Jersey and brought Jersey girl back with me, and all was going according to script until Christmas Eve.

No fault of her own, but she got sick that night, a viral gastroenteritis or stomach virus that had both of us spending our Christmas Eve, our "first of many," sitting on the bathroom floor. The bathroom floor was cool in temperature, offering some relief from the heat that radiated off her feverish body, and most importantly the shortest distance to the commode, where she would intermittently make visits to vomit. I held her in my arms trying to comfort her ill body, all the while wondering how all my plans always seemed to be altered when it came to this relationship. Perhaps it was just not meant to be.

Christmas day I had planned a meal, but much of it was not eaten. Though the vomiting had stopped for Jersey girl, the pain of disappointment for me lingered on. I was not disappointed with her but rather at the fact that no matter how hard I seemed to try to make our relationship work, either I would do something to damage it, or some distraction would occur that made our relationship not possible. That evening I drove Jersey girl home for the last time.

Several months passed before the realization hit that our relationship was over. The spring season had arrived, and with it a fresh start. I had never really dated before, going from one long-term commitment to the next. I quickly realized I was not missing anything. The dates came and went, but at twenty-seven years, many of my female peers had been married or had children. I was not against that, but I was not looking for an instant family, either.

The summer ended as the spring began, with me a single man just finishing my first year of family-medicine residency training. I was beginning to become frustrated with the dating scene and felt that I honestly could not fall in love again. The emotional roller coaster I had ridden with Jersey girl had taken all the passion out of me. I struggled to let anyone get close to me, making some excuse as to why a particular person was not right for me. The woman who would become my wife experienced this behavior firsthand; lucky for me, she was a very persistent young woman.

THE POSTER BOY
BECOMES THE ONE

One day in September 2001, while working in the family-medicine office, I was approached by a medical assistant, or MA, who worked in the residence office. She also worked in the phlebotomy lab, the so-called vampires of the hospital. The phlebotomists were the workers who were given the inglorious task of drawing blood from patients at all hours of the day, undoubtedly the most disliked employees of the hospital because nobody likes needles.

The MA came up to me and told me she worked with a woman in the phlebotomy lab who wanted to meet me and had asked that she give me her number. I was a twenty-seven-year-old single male who was struggling with the dating game; this was one I did not have to think about. "Sure, I'll take her number." I had never met the person whose number I then held in my hands, but at that moment, what did I have to lose?

I had never called a blind phone number before, but when I did, I was greeted with a voice mail. I stated who I was and that I had received her phone number from a mutual coworker. I left my phone number and figured if I did not hear anything back from the unknown woman, I still had not lost anything. I hung up the phone after leaving my message and did not think about the phone call until later that day, when I went to the hospital cafeteria. I descended the staircase, as I had many times in the past, to enter the backside of the cafeteria.

As I opened the door and walked into the cafeteria, I noticed a group of women at a round table eating their dinner. They were all in scrubs, denoting they were hospital employees of some variety. I did not know anyone at the table, but for a moment one of the women stood out to me. She was sitting facing the door I had entered, wearing green scrubs and smiling. I had the strangest feeling that the person I had called earlier in the day and left a message with was the woman I noticed at the table. As quickly as the thought entered my mind, I dismissed it as a crazy thought, or perhaps it was a wish, as the woman was very attractive.

I proceeded to get my food from the grill line and checked out at the register like normal, noticing nothing else that was out of the ordinary. I ate my dinner rapidly, which was the normal tendency I had when eating at the hospital, as time was never plentiful. I returned to my clinical duties to finish up the workday.

That evening, September 20, 2001, I received a phone call from a woman I had never talked to before. It was the woman I had called earlier in the day and left a message with; her name was Melissa Peters. She stated she was working when I had called and had missed my call because she could not have her phone with her in the hospital.

Recalling my strange yet brief epiphany as I was walking down the cafeteria entrance stairs and saw a table of female employees eating dinner, I took what I thought was a chance. I asked her if she had worn green scrubs to work that day. She confirmed that she had. She asked how I knew that, and at the risk of sounding crazy, I explained how I had a feeling that I saw her, yet I was not sure, as I had never met her before. I proceeded to admit to her that I had a sensation that the person in the green scrubs was her, the person I had called earlier in the day.

She started to laugh; I felt silly and thought the conversation was headed downhill. It was a feeling that did not last, as she told me that she was indeed the person I thought was her. She admitted she saw me too, though she knew what I looked like. She made a confession of her own next. She told me that she saw me enter the cafeteria, and at the encouragement of the women at her table, she got up and followed me into the food area. She had already bought her dinner and was full, so she just grabbed a drink and got behind me in line, but I never noticed any of this. She admitted that she got nervous and did not say anything to me, allowing me to pay and leave with what she thought was a lost opportunity. When she returned to her table, her coworkers teased her that she had blown her opportunity. It was not until later in the day, when her workday was done, that she found out that I had called her already. Perhaps she had one more opportunity, she thought.

We both got a good laugh out of our stories. She asked me how I knew it was her at the table in the cafeteria, but I had no answer. It was a strong belief that was transient but based on nothing factual, and to this day I cannot explain it. I asked her how she knew me. She laughed again, something I would soon realize was a common thing for her—she loved to laugh. She admitted that I was the poster boy.

The poster boy? What did that mean? It did not sound like a flattering title. York Hospital is a five-hundred-plus-bed community teaching hospital with numerous residency training programs. Each year to help staff with the recognition of all the residents, a poster with pictures of all the residents was printed and posted throughout the hospital.

Melissa's phlebotomy office had one such poster. She explained that she was single and scanned the poster, pointed to my picture, and said, "I'll take that one." One of her coworkers, who also worked in the family-medicine office as a medical assistant, told her that she knew and worked with me. That is when Melissa made the bold move of offering her phone number to her coworker.

We talked about the typical things people talking for the first time discuss. The conversation was going very well until hints about her age led me to get spooked. In a week, I was turning twenty-eight years. She did not come out and tell me her age, but simple math told me she was going to turn twenty, interestingly also in a week—in fact, one day after my birthday.

That meant she was still a teenager, a reality that almost led to there not being a first date. Not only had I never seen her, but she was much younger than I was. I was concerned that there would be too big a maturity gap. I realized that our conversation had gone so well that I decided that we should at least meet and see how we interacted in person. I knew from experience that a great conversation on the phone does not always mean a great first impression in a person, but, once again, I had nothing to lose, so we arranged to get ice cream at a small shop that made their own.

The day of the first date with my wife was to be was a special day, not solely because it was our first date, for I did not know before our date that we would ultimately be married. Another event happened earlier in the day that made an impression; I met the man whose autobiography steered me into medicine. I had finished my intern year just a few months earlier, and now Dr. Benjamin Carson was speaking at a local church, conveniently a block from my apartment. After listening to his speech, much of which anyone who'd read his book, *Gifted Hands*, would recognize, we remained for an autograph session. I took along my copy and presented it to the inspirational figure of my youth.

I was both excited and nervous, knowing I did not have much time to talk to him, yet wanting him to know how his story had inspired me. To achieve this goal, I wrote him a thank-you card with a brief message, stating that his life had influenced mine. I do not know if he ever read the card, but his response to my thank-you was less than touching. He shook my hand with a pen in his, did not make eye contact, then proceeded to spell my name wrong. I left the table deflated.

Later that day, I had a date with Melissa. It was our first, but it almost did not happen. We had planned to meet and go to a local ice cream stand. Everyone in York considered the local shop the best place to get ice cream. Melissa arrived at my apartment, but the day was stressful for her, as she had a moment when she did not know if she was going to make it for our first date.

She had been at the mall early in the day, and when she was about to leave, she realized she'd locked her keys in her car. Panicked, she was assisted by the police in getting her car opened. When I heard the ring of the doorbell, I descended the stairs to my apartment door. I had talked for a couple of hours to the woman on the other side of the door, and although I had seen her briefly in the cafeteria, I did not know that was her, so when I opened the door, I saw my future wife for the first time.

It would be romantic and like a fairy tale if I said it was love at first sight and that her beauty took my breath away, but that would not be completely honest. As I walked down the stairwell to greet Melissa, all I could think about was why I had agreed to go on a date with a nineteen-year-old. I will admit that when I opened the door and saw her pretty face with its larger-than-life smile, I chuckled inside that maybe age would not matter after all.

We arrived at Handles. The line typically was long, but this particular day it did not matter. Melissa and I had driven together, and the conversation flowed easily, making time fly by. It was a warm day for the end of September, which my wife and I joke was in my favor. We both ordered ice cream cones, mine with my favorite strawberry cheesecake. We stood outside the shop, as it did not have an inside, and continued sharing about ourselves. I soon realized that Melissa's ice cream had dripped a rather large amount on the front of her red shirt. I gathered several napkins and awkwardly tried to help wipe the ice cream from her chest. It gave us a good laugh and plenty to talk about for years to come.

A week later Melissa and I celebrated our twentieth and twenty-eighth birthdays, on September 26 and 27. I planned to have a birthday party, so I invited Melissa and some other friends. A special present was the presence of my sister Nicole, the eldest of my three sisters. It was special in that she lived in Florida, and we had not spoken for over five years, mostly due to my stubbornness.

When I left home to attend college, I assumed my sister Nicole would take over the responsibility of caring for our two youngest siblings. It was an incorrect assumption. It was not fair or appropriate to believe this would become Nicole's task just because I had done it. When I left for college in 1991, Nicole was only ten years old, too young to become a caregiver for anyone, never mind two toddlers. The responsibility was still there, and it must have been too much for her, because she ran away from home to live with Mrs. H, who provided her with a room with a few bells and whistles; my parents could not compete. What angered me was that I perceived Nicole as abandoning our sisters and was even more upset that Mrs. H would encourage her leaving her family. I refused to talk to either of them about it, and five years went by very quickly.

That night my sister and I reconnected while I got to know a young woman who would become my soul mate. Nicci acquired the nickname Corona due to her indulgence in the Mexican cerveza that holds its name. My sister no longer consumes alcohol, and I have always wondered how much that night had to do with her abstinence.

I learned two important things that night as a result of my sister drinking too much beer: that my sister should not drink at all and that Melissa's heart was a compassionate one. I am not sure it was what my sister had in mind when she said she was going to screen Melissa as a potential girlfriend of mine, but the majority of the night saw them together. My sister knelt before the porcelain throne while Melissa held her hair back from the emesis that filled the toilet bowl. I still look back at that night as a sign of Melissa's character. There she was, at a party celebrating the birthday of the man she just met a week earlier, hoping to win him over, and instead of spending time with him, she was at the side of another in need.

The first three months of our relationship were not the smoothest for one in its honeymoon phase. I admittedly battled with the age difference. I was going to dance clubs with friends before Melissa and I had met, and I continued to go out with them after. I wanted to bring my new girlfriend with us, but Melissa was not of an age to enter the clubs. It became an issue I struggled with, and the few friends I had did not make it any easier on me.

I let the age difference get in the way of our relationship ever taking off. I cannot recount how many times I broke up with Melissa, though I am sure she can. There were many such times, lasting only days before we would restart our relationship. I never had a legitimate reason for wanting to end our relationship, and trust me, in those early days, I tried to find one. Melissa was intelligent, funny, loving, caring, and never seemed to be in a bad mood. There was no reason for anyone not to like her and that she chose me to be with should not have taken as long as it did to register in my stubborn brain. It had taken three months and one memorable talk on the balcony of my second-floor apartment in York, Pennsylvania, before I realized that I would not find a better woman to spend the rest of my life with.

It was a cool late-fall afternoon, minutes before sunset, when Melissa and I were having another discussion about our relationship. As always, it was me trying to end it, and Melissa asking why it should end. I never had an answer that made any logical sense, and Melissa would not take an answer that didn't. I finally asked questions of my own, questions that would end the breakup roller coaster I had been subjecting Melissa to ride for months.

"What is this? What do you think we are? Why will you not just let us end?" I yelled.

"I think you are 'the one,'" Melissa replied with a soft, confident tone as she walked away and left me to ponder her statement.

Several days passed until the reality of what Melissa had said computed in my stubborn brain: you are "the one." Was she "the one"? It was the natural question to ask. No matter how hard or from what direction I attempted to analyze the question, the answer was the same. For months before meeting her, I had some one-date encounters, and with each, I found something about her that prevented a second rendezvous.

Then along came Melissa, a blind encounter. Although I struggled with the age difference, I could find no reason not to believe she could be the one. I had fallen in love with her, and there was no amount of logic that could change that. What was there not to love?

I realized that my chances with her were about to end, and she could have any man she wanted, yet she wanted me. I almost let her go—or rather pushed her away. Instead, it has been fourteen years, and two children later, and we are more in love today than we were then. I would be lying, though, if I said it was all rosy after that fall evening on my balcony.

LOSING EVERYTHING... AGAIN!

My third and final year of family-medicine resi-dency had begun, and I could see the home stretch. I was about to begin my final rotation in obstetrics, and although I knew I was not going to deliver babies as part of my clinical practice after I graduated, I did thoroughly enjoy it and thus sought a personal goal of graduating with the most deliver-ies in my graduation class. It was a wonderfully iso-lated rotation out in Chambersburg, Pennsylvania, where I had no competing residents to fight for de-liveries with.

The experience one received was completely dependent on one's effort. I sprinted out of the blocks with eagerness and began piling up the number of deliveries rapidly. I would work side by side with the midwife on call during the night hours to make sure I did not miss any deliveries. During the middle of my rotation, however, I started to burn out. I began missing deliveries as I struggled to get out of bed. I reached out to the family-medicine OB director at the time, and I explained my goals and how I had started out so well, but now something was holding me back.

We concluded through honesty and candidness that I was suffering from depression. She suggested I start a medication to combat the mood disorder. I felt I needed to do something, and through our discussions, I gained a trust in my faculty mentor that I previously had not had. I agreed to initial pharmacologic management; I was going to take the medication.

I had trialed antidepressants in the past but never stuck with them, mainly due to personal denial that I needed them. This medication, Effexor XR, was a new medicine in a new class of medications, and for the first time, it was me who was reaching out for help. I felt confident that it was going to be the medication that changed my life. It did not disappoint; my life was soon changed, but not in the way I had anticipated.

As a family-medicine resident, call nights are long but are times when much learning happens. It was September of my third and final year of residency, ten months until graduation. I felt comfortable in my skills and was eager to start a new chapter in my life, planning to enter private practice as a family doctor. My night of call reminded me that I had still much to learn, as I had a very interesting patient who needed to be admitted to the hospital with the weakness of his arms and legs. His diagnosis was Guillain-Barré syndrome, a neurologic disease of the autoimmune system. I was very excited about the case and was eager to share what I had learned with my fellow residents in our daily conference, called morning report.

Typically, morning report is a time that the on-call resident has the responsibility to present an interesting and educational case to the group. As an innate teacher, I researched most of the night as much as I could about Guillain-Barré syndrome and prepared what I believed was a very good teaching session. As 8:00 a.m. approached, I grew increasingly excited and ready to pass on the knowledge I had gained the night before. I had not slept, but I was energized.

Morning report cases were typically presented routinely. My learning and teaching style was not by this routine. I wanted to engage and stimulate the audience, awakening the young minds in the room first thing in the morning. The leader of the morning report, a second-year resident, had a strong objection to my plans. I was standing at the dry erase board with a red marker in hand, eagerly anticipating the start of the morning.

Little did I know or realize that the simple act of writing on the board was against the rules. I was told that I could not be the one writing on the board, as it was her job to lead morning report. I attempted to explain that I had a very good case to present and that I had spent all night preparing the case in a fashion that I believed would engage the audience.

My words would fall on deaf ears. The stubbornness on both sides boiled over as I submitted, tossed the marker in the air, and refused to be a part of the morning presentation if not leading it. Feeling my anger level rising exponentially and knowing that if I did not remove myself from this escalating scenario, I would say something I would regret, I walked away to my desk, which was in a separate room, approximately ninety yards away.

Ninety yards was not far enough. I was not aware initially that the female resident I was fighting with had decided to follow me to my desk. As a stood at my desk, I heard her yell, "You are so immature, Jason!" I had had it with her, and without any thought, I snapped my body around to confront her latest verbal attack.

Immaturity is one thing, and I agree we both were guilty, but my actions and words that followed were inappropriate and vulgar. Standing about twenty feet away, I had feelings of intense anger and disgust for the person I was staring at with burning eyes. Before I could even think about what I was doing, the words were out, and the hand was placed in an anatomic area not fit for any workplace or otherwise.

"Suck this!" I yelled as my right hand grabbed my genitalia. The room, occupied by a handful of other coresidents, became deadly quiet. The resident whom my disgust was aimed at stood with an astonished look on her face, and without saying another word left the room, leaving me to feel the weight of what had just transpired as the atmosphere became suffocating. I immediately knew my actions were wrong, and I regretted the moment, but it was done, and I could not take it back. All I wanted was to be left alone with time to calm myself down and regroup my emotions.

They say be careful what you wish for. I would never see that resident again, and I would get plenty of time alone to calm down, but not in the manner I was looking for. The resident I had the conflict with reported me to faculty, and before I could return to work the next day, I was put on a two-week suspension, although it was just a formality. The suspension turned into my termination from the program, despite my letter to the faculty detailing my version of the conflict. I am sure I did not help myself when they asked me to write a letter of apology to the female resident, and I refused. However, I have always believed the faculty had their minds made up as soon as the incident had happened.

There was little if anything that I could have done to keep my position in the program. The faculty deemed my conduct sexual harassment, instant grounds for dismissal. I have heard time and again what other people thought I could not do or accomplish, never finding it my style to listen to them, but the words of one faculty to me on the day I was dismissed from the residency program have left an emotional scar that remains over fifteen years later.

"Jason, after what you did, you are not a good enough person to be a doctor."

The words were from a senior faculty member, a supposed mentor. I understood my actions were unprofessional, and I expected some form of disciplinary action, but for them to release me from my duties just ten months from completion and to hear those words—at that moment I started to cry.

Sternness prevailed on the other end of the table, and at the conclusion of our meeting, three security guards escorted me off hospital grounds.

There is little more humbling than having your friends and colleagues watch as you are shamefully removed from your place of employment by security. I got into my car and slowly pulled out of York Hospital parking lot, wondering about, among many things, whether I would soon be living out of my car again.

Instead of consulting a lawyer, I tried to appeal through the hospital appeals process. I was granted a hearing with a committee that I assumed would be impartial, an assumption that could not have been more incorrect. As I entered the room, several doctors sat surrounding an oblong table. Each member of the committee avoided eye contact with me. They did not need to; they all knew who I was.

I am sure I do not recall every member of the committee sitting at the table that day, but those I do remember include my former chief resident, a fellow third-year resident just weeks prior, adjunct members of the faculty for the department of family medicine, and the director of pediatrics, also a faculty leader in the department of family medicine. The only non-family-medicine-affiliated members of the appeals committee were two unfortunate third-year internal-medicine residents, both of whom I had worked with recently on an ICU elective. I did not have an impartial jury, to say the least. Feeling defeated before the meeting even started, I offered little in the way of remorse or hope as I was awkwardly questioned by the committee.

In the end, the result was as expected: I lost the appeal and was an unemployed doctor once again.

Losing medicine for the second time in four years is not a good formula for the management of depression. My psyche and my pride had been damaged yet again, not because I could not provide compassionate, competent medical care to my patients, but because I lost control of my temper and acted most unprofessionally. This termination of my medical training affected me the most, for I felt that this must have been a sign. Perhaps the faculty was correct. Was I not good enough, not a good enough person to be a physician? I did not want to self-reflect on the question, let alone answer it. As I had in the past, I attempted to solve the problem the only way I knew how: I let King Depression take over, and I tried to sleep all my troubles and worry away.

I had never been sure if my girlfriend, Melissa, completely comprehended how I felt, losing something that meant the world to me, but I know she was very aware of how my hibernation status made her feel. It was painful for her. I neglected her and refused to see her or answer any calls from her—but it was not just her, it was everyone. I wanted no part of the world outside of my bedroom. I got up to eat a bowl of cereal or a couple of pieces of toast on occasion, answered the call of nature when needed, but that was the extent of my daily adventures. Soon I needed to face a harsh reality, though: no work meant no pay, and no income meant I would soon be back on the street and homeless. A person with a healthier mental state would be alarmed by this fact, but it just made me sleep even more.

A month or two went by with little change. I felt no hope. Making matters worse, I lost my health insurance, and the new antidepressant I was started on a few months prior was expensive, and, well, a roof over my head took priority. Being honest, I had truly felt that the new medication was partially responsible for my outburst on my final day of work in early September 2002. I made the decision myself to stop the Effexor XR shortly after. My life was headed in only one direction, one I would not have wished for anyone.

It was midfall 2002 when I first saw the emotional strength of Melissa. I am sure it was not a decision she made in haste, but it was one that provided me a needed crossroad in life, yet it was still my choice as to which direction I would follow.

I was awakened from my slumber by the front door of my apartment opening. Determined and firm footsteps climbed the staircase to the living room. Unable to enter my bedroom, as I had locked the door, Melissa sat and wrote a note, a note left with a bottle of medication. The message was simple yet strong: "If you ever want to see me again, start taking your medicine and get your life back together." I took the Effexor that night, and although my life was not back together that night, it was on its way on what was and remains a long, continuous challenge.

As a young man with a large chip on his shoulder, I often felt I was fighting the battles of life on my own, and any success I had was that of my own doing. Another life lesson was in the making from the aftermath of my release from residency training. As feared, without an income, I soon lost my apartment and was looking at not having a place to live other than my car.

Melissa Peters and her family saved the day again. I felt like I hardly knew Melissa's oldest sister, Jennifer, and her husband, Brett. Sure, I had been dating Melissa for a year and a half, but we were not getting married soon, and I rarely spoke with Jennifer or Brett. How could I expect them just to let me move in with them?

To my surprise, they seemed not to have a problem with me occupying a spare bedroom in their home. I spent six months in a home that provided security and hope. I have never been able to thank Jennifer and Brett enough for their generosity. The act of kindness arguably saved my life in many ways, and though I have never voiced it enough over the years since, I am well aware of the impact it had and will never forget it.

Soon after life started to look up, I applied and was accepted for a job as an adjunct faculty for an Anatomy and Physiology night course at Harrisburg Community College, Lancaster Campus. I instructed mostly nontraditional students with an interest in the health sciences. It was my first time as a course instructor, but I enjoyed it tremendously, having always had a passion for normal anatomy and especially physiology. I prepared lecture and lab material and originated exams and quizzes for the course.

It was as difficult to work as it had been the first time teaching, and I had no resources to draw from. I was extremely happy to teach, however, something I always knew I would do in my career, just not in this manner. I soon realized that being accepted as an adjunct faculty member was therapeutic for me as well. It forced me into engaging my mind once again, and my mood reflected the positive impact. However, I knew that as much as I needed it and as much as I enjoyed it, teaching college courses was not what I was destined to do with my life.

ONE-LAST-CHANCE
DOCTOR

I started to believe again that despite what my previous faculty in York, Pennsylvania, had said about me, I was a good person and one just as worthy as another to be a doctor. With this newfound confidence, I looked for training programs that needed a second-year family-medicine resident. Although I was in my third and final year of residency when I was terminated, guidelines set by the American College of Graduate Medical Education state residents must complete the last two years of their training in the same institution. This meant that not only would I have to finish my third and final year that I had started, but I would have to repeat my second year of training as well.

Although this was not the ideal plan, I was in no position to complain when, after several failed interviews with various family-medicine residency programs, the Medical College of Georgia gave me another chance. I was accepted into their training program as a second-year family-medicine resident. I knew nothing about Augusta, Georgia, other than that it was the host of the Masters golf tournament, but I was eager to learn all about it, and deep down also very happy to have the opportunity to move back to Georgia. Only one more task was left to make my move to Georgia definite, a task I was not looking forward to as I feared what the reaction would be, but it had to be done. This was potentially my last chance in medicine; I could not let it pass. Melissa must know that I was moving to Georgia for two years.

When I shared with Melissa that I had found a residency program to accept me, she was very happy for me. When I told her the program was in Georgia, I watched her expression change to one of concern. What would this mean for our relationship? She was in college completing courses for nursing school. She was as committed to finishing her education as I was determined to finish my training.

The uncertainty of a long-distance relationship made the moment uncomfortable for both of us. I was attempting not to seem too happy, and Melissa was trying to seem happier than she felt. In my mind, however, the choice was made. I was going to Georgia; nothing could be done or said to change my mind. My priority was completing my training, so I could practice medicine as a career. Melissa, being the loving and compassionate woman she is, never tried convincing me to stay. She supported me as only she could, though I knew inside she was scared that she might be losing "the one."

I completed my residency training over the next two years at the Medical College of Georgia in scenic Augusta. In retrospect, it was a defining time for my relationship with Melissa. The distance could have separated us more than just geographically, yet somehow we made it through. We both kept very busy; Melissa was in nursing school and I—well, I was just trying my best not to be released from my third residency program.

The introduction of two new things into my life balanced me, allowing me to finish my training. I started playing tennis at a local public tennis club. I would take group lessons and soon joined an USTA (United States Tennis Association) league at a beginner level. It was just the break from medicine I needed. It was also a great way to meet people away from work.

I also started moonlighting in a rural emergency room, working twelve-hour shifts as the sole night-time doctor. Initially, my motive for working in the emergency room was to finance the frequent flights to have Melissa visit me. We were fairly successful in seeing each other every six to eight weeks. It did not take long for me to realize the invaluable medical experience I was getting from the extra work in the emergency room.

Working as the sole doctor, alongside one nurse, taking care of anything and everything that came into our medical center, was very intimidating. There was a steep learning curve that quickly helped grow my confidence in my medical skills. However, as life so often does, a tragic early morning event brought my ego back to reality. His panic-stricken face still haunts my thoughts.

A young man entered the emergency room struggling for breath. He was suffering from an asthma attack. He was immediately brought back to an exam room. As the nurse and I were evaluating him, he began begging to be intubated. He wanted us to place a breathing tube into his airway and connect him to a ventilator. I momentarily froze. I had never had a patient ask to be intubated before.

I watched as the amount of effort it was taking Mr. Jackson to breathe increased. I agreed that intubation was the appropriate next step. I called for the respiratory therapist in the hospital to assist. I observed as the respiratory therapist struggled with the intubation. At one point, I attempted to place the artificial airway myself but also failed. I knew time was of the essence. We needed to secure the gentleman's airway quickly. We ran out of time. Mr. Jackson did not survive.

I had never lost a patient before. Realizing the fate of the young man who had come in pleading for our help, I lost control of my emotions. Walking out of the exam room, I threw my stethoscope across the room. Finding the nearest chair, I sat down, put my head in my hands, and started to cry. It was my responsibility to save the young man's life, yet I had failed. I decided at that moment it would be my last shift in an emergency room.

I would succeed in completing my residency training, but I definitely had to battle my way to the finish line. Many of the faculty found me unteachable and difficult to work with. I still had a large chip on my shoulder and agree that I was a very difficult learner.

My care of patients was never a question; rather it was the lack of professionalism I displayed toward fellow colleagues. I was told once that several of the faculty wanted me removed from the program. Fortunately for me, my program director did not agree, although I did make it difficult for him, I am sure. One of the most positive things ever said to me came from him. He was a very honest person who discussed with me my professionalism issues. He also told me I was one of the brightest residents he had ever trained and that it would be a great loss to family medicine if I was not to complete my training. After that meeting I vowed to myself that I would do the best I could to cause as few problems as possible and just get through the program. He believed in me; it was time that I believed in myself also.

Believing in oneself can be difficult when those charged with being your mentors give you negative feedback. Although the conversation with my program director was positive, one with my associate program director was more painful to endure. I had been discussing with her my future plans to be an academic family physician as part of a residency program, where I could teach residents and medical students. The response was blunt.

"Jason, you will never be faculty. You are just not faculty material." She advised that I go into private practice and give up on any chances of being faculty in the future. I walked away from her office unable to comprehend our conversation.

All I knew was that I did not believe her, and I was not ever going to abandon my dream. I knew what I wanted to do and fought too hard to listen to her advice. I was going to follow my plan after residency, which was to enter private practice for five years. After working hard to solidify my medical skills and knowledge, I would transition into academic medicine as a residency faculty.

A FOUNDATION IS BUILT, YET TESTED

With most of my formative years being in Florida and Georgia, I had little desire to return to a northern state. However, if I wanted the girl, a return to Pennsylvania was necessary. Melissa had one year left in nursing school, and with her strong family ties, I knew a transition south was unlikely. I was not very eager to return to York, Pennsylvania. I had not emotionally recovered from my departure two years earlier. Melissa and I found a compromise. Carlisle, Pennsylvania, is a borough in Cumberland County, east of Harrisburg, with a population of just under nineteen thousand. Home to Dickinson College and the US Army War College, Carlisle is rich in history and, most importantly, was forty miles from Melissa's family. It was in Carlisle that I would begin my medical career, finally achieving what I was told I would never achieve.

In the summer of 2005, I began working with a group of three other family physicians in a private practice serving the Carlisle community. The moment I met the two partners of the practice, I knew I would be welcomed into the group and supported as I transitioned from learner to independent provider. I was not disappointed, as I spent seven years with the practice, leaving only to pursue academic career goals.

My time in Carlisle was marked by tremendous professional and personal growth. Many of the previous barriers to my success had been overcome, and now Melissa and I were finally together. We moved into our first house together and married on July 8, 2006. With a supportive wife and friends for colleagues, I focused on my medical career. I was soon seeing between twenty and twenty-five patients a day, caring for them in the hospital and the office. I acquired a patient panel rather quickly and got to know my patients well. Many families remain in my thoughts, but there is one patient who will be in my heart forever.

A fifty-year-old woman who appeared much older due to her habits was hospitalized with an infection in the colon called Clostridium difficile colitis or C. diff. I would get regular calls from the nursing staff stating that my patient was in the bathroom smoking. One time she was found outside squatting between cars in the parking lot smoking cigarettes.

I got so upset with my patient's behavior that I went into the hospital room one evening and grabbed the box of cigarettes sitting on the stand by the bed and ripped the remainder of the cigarettes in half as the patient watched with a surprisingly calm manner. I left the room feeling victorious. I should have known better. The next day the nurse informed me that after I left the room my patient retrieved a new pack of cigarettes and started smoking in the room: patient, 1; Dr. Ramirez, 0. I called the patient Mom.

My mother had been living in Florida where she had remarried and was sober for several years until her disease of addiction took control of her life again. She had gone to her primary-care doctor for headaches and was put on a narcotic for pain control. That was all it took, and she was hooked once again. Feeling guilty and depressed about her relapse, she unsuccessfully attempted suicide.

Upon learning about her struggles, I decided I was going to be the savior once again. I moved my mother, who needed much convincing, up to Pennsylvania to live with Melissa and me. I helped her detox and attempted the best I could to doctor her depression, migraine headaches, and insomnia. In an effort to control many diseases with one medication, I prescribed her a medication called amitriptyline. Little did I realize my mother had her own plan for its use.

The white van parked outside my house was all that I needed to see. I knew the outcome of the pending conversation before it began. As I got out of my car, a man with a saddened face approached me.

"Dr. Ramirez, my name is Jon. I am from the coroner's office." He explained that my mother was found dead in the backseat of her car, which was parked in the driveway of the gentleman she had been dating. Empty bottles of amitriptyline, with the prescriber's name of Dr. Jason Ramirez, were by her side. Toxicology reports confirmed lethal levels of the drug in her system. My purpose had been to save my mother; instead I gave her the vehicle that ended her journey in life.

The only explanation for my not relapsing into a severe depression was the love and support from my wife and her family. I felt responsible for the death of my mother. Had I not been surrounded by people who cared for me, I am not sure what direction life would have taken me.

A year after the passing of my mother, I came home from work to hear unexpected news from my wife. After my temporary period of hibernation, we learned the news of my wife's pregnancy, and we embraced the future of parenthood. I feared not being a good father. What experience was I to draw from? I determined I would do my very best. We started learning as much as we could by reading parenting books, as most first-time parents do, only to realize later that parenting cannot be scripted.

Our son, Alexander, is undeniably my mini-me, and why should he be anything less? Not only was I partly responsible for his creation, I also assisted in bringing him into the world.

The night my wife went into labor, our midwife was having a busy night, with several mothers in active labor simultaneously. The time came when my wife was ready to push, but the midwife had another patient also ready to deliver. The midwife was noticeably stressed. Melissa offered a solution to the midwife.

"My husband is a family doctor. He can deliver babies." Before I knew it, I was gowned and gloved and positioned in front of my wife in preparation for delivering my firstborn child.

People often marvel at this story and comment that it must have been amazing to deliver my son into the world, although all the credit goes to my wife, as she is the one who delivered him. I just caught him. I readily acknowledge it as a special moment that I will always remember.

However, being a doctor took something away from the experience. As a physician, I went into doctor mode. I visualized the birthing technique and the sequence of events about to happen. I mentally reviewed the potential complications of the birthing process and what I would do if such complications would occur. Before I had a chance to experience any emotions, the delivery was over, and our son was in his mother's arms.

I have no regret about my role in our son's entrance into the world. However, I told Melissa should we have another child, I would be at the head of the bed, holding her hand and sharing the special moment together.

In 2012, I made the difficult decision to leave private practice and enter academic medicine. My plan had always been to teach at a resident level. What made the decision difficult were the strong bonds I had formed with my patients and the people I worked with. However, when an opportunity to join a residency program in Rome, Georgia, arose, I felt the time had come to pursue my longtime goal of being a medical educator.

The transition was difficult for Melissa, as she missed her family in Pennsylvania. Seven months after we had arrived in Georgia, it became obvious to me that we would have to return home. I came home from work one evening to see my son, Alex, wearing a shirt reading, "I am going to be a big brother."

This time I did not hibernate. Despite personally wanting to live in Georgia, I knew Melissa missed her family and was not happy being so far away from them. With the news that we were expecting our second child, I knew what I had to do. I immediately started the job search for faculty positions near home. After several failed attempts, I accepted an offer to join the Department of Family and Community Medicine at the University of Maryland School of Medicine in Baltimore, Maryland. Little did I realize how great an opportunity this would become.

I stood at the head of the bed holding Melissa's hand as Olivia Violet Ramirez entered the world on February 18, 2014. I had been blessed to have had the privilege of assisting in the delivery of my son, and Olivia's birth was also uniquely special. I felt the emotions of being a proud father as I supported my wife in the effort of bringing a child into the world. Our family was complete with one boy and one girl. Life seemed to be perfect. We were back home, and Melissa was happy, which she deserved. She easily transitioned jobs as an emergency-room nurse at the University of Maryland Medical Center. I had found myself at a world-class academic medical center and clinical faculty.

Since joining the faculty at the University of Maryland School of Medicine, I have never been more professionally fulfilled. I have excelled under the guidance of wonderful mentors. My initial position as the director of inpatient medicine was perfect for my interests. In this role, I was responsible for the care of the hospitalized patients of our practice and led the efforts to educate the residents and students on the inpatient service.

In 2017, three and a half years into my tenure at the University of Maryland, I have accepted the challenge of becoming the residency-program director. I am responsible for the training of thirty family-medicine residents. It is an overwhelming responsibility, but one I look forward to doing for many years.

IF I CAN DO IT, YOU CAN DO IT TOO

A young man carrying a large chip on his shoulder and not worthy of being a doctor transitioned to a humble man charged with leading a family-medicine residency program at a prestigious institution. I often reflect on the early years of my life and wonder how I ever got to where I am today. I hear the words of my medical-school interviewer: "Why are you not on the street, addicted to drugs, in prison, or dead?" My father used to tell me as a child that there were two ways to do things in life: the easy way and the hard way. I have to agree with him when he said I always seemed to choose the hard way.

The irony is I give much credit to my parents. I have never considered myself gifted intellectually. I felt I had to work a little harder than others to achieve the same goals. My parents worked extremely hard in life to keep our family together. They may not have been textbook parents, but they showed us love and shielded us from as much as they could. I am sure they did not realize it, but they were teaching me a valuable life lesson.

Hard work is the only way to succeed in life. I had always been an average student until I decided to do better. I began working harder to be the best I could be in school, and it translated into instant success. Granted, my motive was not the best. I wanted to get good grades to improve, of course, but what I wanted was to do better than all the other students. Although my way of thinking drove me to work hard and allowed me to reach high levels of academic success, it did not help my social life. As a consequence, I was never very popular among my peers, nor did I form any long-lasting friendships during my college, medical school, or residency training.

This mentality continued until I got into medical school, and it undoubtedly played a large role in my getting accepted. I still wanted to be better than others in medical school, but now I was competing with the smartest students around. I initially held my own, but depression took control and would dominate my life for years to come. Depression is a chronic disease that affects the lives of many individuals and their families. The disease nearly destroyed my life on several occasions. Somehow, I was fortunate to overcome the consequences of my depression each time. Each time I was knocked down by life's stiff jab to the chin, I stumbled to my feet before the count of ten.

I used to believe I was getting up by my own strength, but now acknowledge I was assisted by the hands of others. Without the love and support of the few people in my life, I may not have been able to get up off the canvas. Stability in my life, however, did not come until I accepted the unconditional love of my wife, Melissa.

Melissa became and remains my foundation in life. Without her, I never would have achieved the life I now enjoy. She has blessed me with two beautiful children, who have further stabilized my reason for existing. Once fearful of having children, I now strive to be the best father I can be. I constantly worry that I am not as good a parent as I could be, but I do my best to be there for my daughter and son.

Though I have not shared my personal story often in my professional career, there have been a few times where it had assisted in the care of a patient.

One particular patient will always stand out in my memory. Ms. Jones was a thin African American woman in her early forties, although she appeared much older. Four years before I met her, she had been hospitalized for a month with complaints of severe, unrelenting abdominal pain, anorexia, nausea, and vomiting. She was treated with nutrition through a feeding tube because she could not tolerate anything by mouth. She had received an exhaustive diagnostic evaluation and was seen by multiple specialists, yet no cause of her symptoms was identified. She stayed in the hospital for four weeks. Ms. Jones would state that she spontaneously improved and was discharged with no answers.

While I was attending the adult inpatient medical service, Ms. Jones was readmitted with a similar issue. She communicated that she had been well since the previous admission four years earlier. I witnessed her malnourished body as it lay motionless in bed, interrupted only by paroxysms of pain and emesis. Numerous laboratory tests and imaging studies were ordered, gastroenterology was consulted, and an esophagogastroduodenoscopy was performed, yet all results returned normal. We still had no answer for Ms. Jones. With knowledge of Ms. Jones's social history of problems with intravenous heroin addiction, my resident team pleaded with me to consider that our patient was malingering. Though malingering was a possibility, I believed our patient was truly suffering.

Days passed, and she remained unable to eat. I contemplated the need for total parental nutrition again. The voices of my senior residents echoed louder each day: "There is nothing wrong with her; she just wants narcotics." Feeling the frustration of having no improvement and no answer to my patient's complaints, I went to Ms. Jones to confront her about the only remaining possibility. I placed a chair by the bedside of Ms. Jones, grabbed her hand, and told her I had tried the best I could to find an answer but that I had failed. She squeezed my hand back and said, "I know you have tried your best."

A silence followed as I searched for the next words to say. Neither of us spoke for what was only seconds but felt like an hour. The silence was broken when I asked her if she thought any of her symptoms could be from heroin withdrawal. The conversation that followed changed both of our lives.

"What do you know about the pain of withdrawal?" her words were harsh.

"Personally, nothing, Ms. Jones; I have never gone through the pains of withdrawal," I responded, and more silence followed.

"I do know the pain of being a child who watched his parents suffer, though," I explained. "My parents too suffered from heroin addiction. I have seen them not only in pain from withdrawal but imprisoned, near death from overdose, and so desperate for money for their next buy that they stole from family and friends. My family and I have been homeless, living out of our car or homeless shelters. I have seen the pain in my mother's eyes as she felt like she was a failure as a mother to her four children."

"You have been through all that?" she asked as her eyes met mine for the first time. "Then you do know. It is not easy; addiction destroys your entire life and everyone in it."

I simply nodded.

Ms. Jones and I talked for over two hours, and in that time, she discussed her battle with addiction and how hard it was to get through the withdrawal stage. There were similar stories of suffering, hunger, depression, and alienation by family and friends. Ms. Jones started to cry again. Displaying vulnerability and humility, she explained to me that she had been trying to improve her life. She started taking a medication called suboxone and was doing well until she was forced to stop due to financial constraints. She began living in fear that she would relapse and return to the streets in search of relief. As we concluded our confessions, Ms. Jones sat up from her bed, gave me a gentle hug, and then said, "Thank you for sharing the story of your parents. I think I'm hungry. I would like to eat dinner now."

Ms. Jones ate a regular meal that evening. The next day she was discharged from the hospital with a great appetite, a script for suboxone provided by assistance from our case-management team, and close follow-up in the substance-abuse clinic. I never saw Ms. Jones in the hospital again.

My encounter with Ms. Jones encouraged me to share my life struggles with others. My purpose is to provide inspiration and hope to people who may feel they have none. I am not a special person with special powers; I just believe that if I can succeed, anyone can.

Life can be brutal, yet it is not hopeless. Barriers such as poverty, addiction, and depression are real and overwhelming. We must dare to dream big, and when barriers seem too big to overcome, we must try harder. Many times we may feel we are alone and have to do everything on our own. I used to feel that way, but with maturity, I realized the truth.

I did not do it on my own, nor could I have. There are people who influence our lives every day, and we never notice. Embrace humanity and allow others to help; it makes life easier. We should not all feel like we must do it the hard way.

Jason Ramirez, MD, studied at Emory University and Drexel University School of Medicine. He now works as the director of the family-medicine residency program at the University of Maryland School of Medicine. Ramirez lives with his family in Baltimore, Maryland. He has a wife and two children.